H E A T H

LANGUAGE ARTS

HEATH
LANGUAGE ARTS

Nicholas Falletta
Merrily P. Hansen, Ed.D.

D.C. Heath and Company

Lexington, Massachusetts • Toronto

Acknowledgments

Program Concept and Development: **Falletta Associates, Inc.**
Executive Editor: Kathleen Fischer
Editors: Leslie Feierstone Barna, Dorrie Berkowitz, and Mary Ellen Gilbert
Contributing Writers: Marilyn Davis, Nancy O'Rourke, Barbara Reeves, and Susan Schornstein
Design and Production: **Graphic Concern, Inc.**
Design: Stan Konopka
Production Director: Ruth Riley
Cover: Fred Marcellino

The authors and editors have made every effort to trace the ownership of all copyrighted selections found in this book and to make full acknowledgment of their use. Grateful acknowledgment is made to the following authors, publishers, agents, and individuals for their permission to reprint copyrighted materials.

Curtis Brown Ltd.: "Valentine Feelings" from *Moments* by Lee Bennett Hopkins. Reprinted by permission of Curtis Brown Ltd. Copyright © 1975 by Lee Bennett Hopkins.

Marchette Chute: "A Monkey" from *Rhymes About the City*. Copyright 1946 (Macmillan). Renewal 1974. Reprinted by permission of the author.

Coward, McCann & Geoghegan: *Headlines* by Malcolm Hall, text copyright 1973 by Malcolm Hall, abridged and reprinted by permission of Coward, McCann, Geoghegan.

Grosset & Dunlap: "Rhyme" by Elizabeth Coatsworth reprinted by permission of Grosset & Dunlap from *The Sparrow Bush* by Elizabeth Coatsworth, copyright © 1966 by Grosset & Dunlap, Inc.

Harper & Row: "Cynthia in the Snow" (text only) from *Bronzeville Boys and Girls* by Gwendolyn Brooks. Copyright © 1956 by Gwendolyn Brooks Blakely. Reprinted by permission of Harper & Row, Publishers, Inc. "October" (text only) from *Chicken Soup With Rice* by Maurice Sendak. Copyright © 1962 by Maurice Sendak. Reprinted by permission of Harper & Row, Publishers, Inc.

Holiday House: "Labor Day" copyright © 1985 by Myra Cohn Livingston. Reprinted from *Celebrations* by permission of Holiday House.

Houghton Mifflin: *The Magic Porridge Pot* by Paul Galdone. Copyright © 1976 by Paul Galdone. Reprinted by permission of Clarion Books/Ticknor & Fields, a Houghton Mifflin Company.

Myra Cohn Livingston: "Martin Luther King" from *No Way of Knowing Dallas Poems*. Copyright © 1980 Myra Cohn Livingston (A Margaret K. McElderry Book). Reprinted with the permission of Atheneum Publishers, Inc.

Macmillan Publishing Company: Reprinted with permission of Four Winds Press, an imprint of Macmillan Publishing Company from *The Goat in the Rug* by Charles L. Blood and Martin Link. Text, copyright © 1976 by Charles L. Blood and Martin Link.

Modern Curriculum Press: "Necks" from *The Day Is Dancing* by Rowena Bastin Bennett. Copyright © 1948, 1968 by Rowena Bastin Bennett. Reprinted by permission of Modern Curriculum Press, Inc.

Random House Inc./Pantheon Books: "Here She Is" from *Give a Guess* by Mary Britton Miller. Copyright © 1957 by Pantheon Books, Inc. Reprinted by permission of the publisher.

Scott, Foresman & Co.: *Scott, Foresman Beginning Dictionary* by E. L. Thorndike and Clarence L. Barnhart, copyright © 1983. Reprinted by permission of Scott, Foresman & Company.

Western Publishing Company: From *A First Thesaurus* by Harriet Wittels and Joan Greisman © copyright 1985 by Harriet Wittels and Joan Griesman. Reprinted by permission of Western Publishing Company, Inc.

Handwriting models used with permission from Zaner-Bloser *Handwriting: Basic Skills and Application*. Copyright © 1984 Zaner-Bloser, Inc., Columbus, Ohio.

(Acknowledgments continue on page xi.)

International Standard Book Number: 0-669-12379-X

1 2 3 4 5 6 7 8 9 0

CONTENTS

UNIT 1

1

42

76

Grammar, Mechanics, and Usage: Verbs

Practical Language Skills: Vocabulary

Unit Test

UNIT 4

Composition: Personal Narrative

Grammar, Mechanics, and Usage: Nouns

viii

UNIT 6

UNIT 7

Grammar, Mechanics, and Usage: Adjectives and Adverbs

Practical Language Skills: Critical Reading Skills

(*Acknowledgments continued from page iv.*)

Illustrators:

Lynn Adams 4–5, 68–69, 166–167; Kelly Carson 270–273; Penny Carter 78, 128–129, 210 bottom; Gwen Connelly 14–15, 39, 67, 130–131; Olivia Cole 26–27, 44–45, 122–123; Rick Cooley 54–55, 60–61, 201; Carolyn Croll 30, 119, 124–125, 172–173; Susan David 288–289, 298–299; Gail DeLuca 200; Pat and Robin DeWitt 12–13, 151, 194–195, 213; John Dyess 302–303; Len Ebert 31, 38, 46–47, 62, 92–93, 103, 133, 136–137, 158–159, 198–199; Les Gray 58–59, 90–91, 175; Marika Hahn 9, 18–19, 81, 112, 156–157, 182–183, 196–197; Meryl Henderson 22–23, 32–33, 117, 138–139, 160–161, 165; Kristina Juzaitis 25, 64, 79, 80, 82–83, 84, 86–87, 102, 113, 168–169, 210 top, 232; Bryce Lee 11, 153, 220–221, 225; Susan Lexa 278–279; Morissa Lipstein 294–295; Anita Lovitt 24, 66, 134–135, 162–163, 202–203; Diana Magnuson 48–49, 50, 94–95, 97, 147, 148–149, 174, 192–193; Laurie Marks 6–7, 20–21, 100, 188–189, 218–219; Jane McCreary 28–29, 180–181, 217; Lyle Miller 120–121, 154–155, 190–191; Sal Murdocca 264–268; Tom Powers 269, 274; Jan Pyke 296; John Rice 56–57, 98–99, 104–107; Nancy Schill 16–17, 34–37, 52–53, 70–71, 88–89, 132, 170, 205, 234–235, 238; Den Schofield 114–115, 184–185, 187, 222–223, 231; Pat Traub 226–229; Alexandra Wallner 286–287; Lane Yerkes 284–285 top.

Illustrations on pages 280, 281, 282, and 283 from *The Magic Porridge Pot* by Paul Galdone. Copyright © 1976 by Paul Galdone. Reprinted by permission of Clarion Books/Ticknor & Fields, a Houghton Mifflin Company.

Illustration on the bottom of page 285 from *Chicken Soup With Rice* by Maurice Sendak. Copyright © 1962 by Maurice Sendak. Reprinted by permission of Harper & Row, Publishers.

Photographers:

Nubar Alexanian/The Stock Market xiv; The Bettman Archives, Inc. 179; Andrew D. Bernstein/The Stock Market 300 left; John Blaustein/Woodfin Camp & Associates xiv-1; Junebug Clark/Photo Researchers Inc. 111 right; Stephan Collins/Photo Researchers Inc. 301 bottom; Jon Feingersh/The Stock Market 290 left; David Frazier/The Stock Market 144; Lowell J. Georgia/Photo Researchers Inc. 277; F.B. Grunzweig/Photo Researchers Inc. 208 bottom; Chip Henderson/Woodfin Camp & Associates 144–145; Michal Heron 2–3; Richard Hutchings/Photo Researchers Inc. 42, 276; Chris Jones/The Stock Market 291 bottom right; Susan L. Jones/Animals, Animals/Earth Scenes 77; John P. Kelly/The Image Bank 145 top; Russ Kinne/Photo Researchers Inc. 301 top; Ken Lax 275; Joe Munroe/Photo Researchers Inc. 301 middle; Bob O'Shaughnessy/ The Stock Market 291 bottom; Gabe Palmer/The Stock Market 110–111, 290 right, 291 top and middle; Steve Skloot/Photo Researchers Inc. 208–209; Luis Villota/The Stock Market 209 right, 300 right.

The following photographs courtesy of: BG Management Services, Inc.–Geneva, Ohio 305 bottom; Chamber of Commerce– Grand Island Nebraska 304 right; Chamber of Commerce–Pella, Iowa 305 top; Montana Historical Society 63; National Watermelon Association–Cordele, Georgia 304 left and bottom; Philadelphia Museum of Art: The Louise and Walter Arensberg Collection 297; Redwood Empire Association 293, 306.

Composition: Overview

NUTRITION

Grammar, Mechanics, and Usage: The Sentence

MUSIC LESSONS

Practical Language Skills: Speaking and Listening

MAKING THINGS

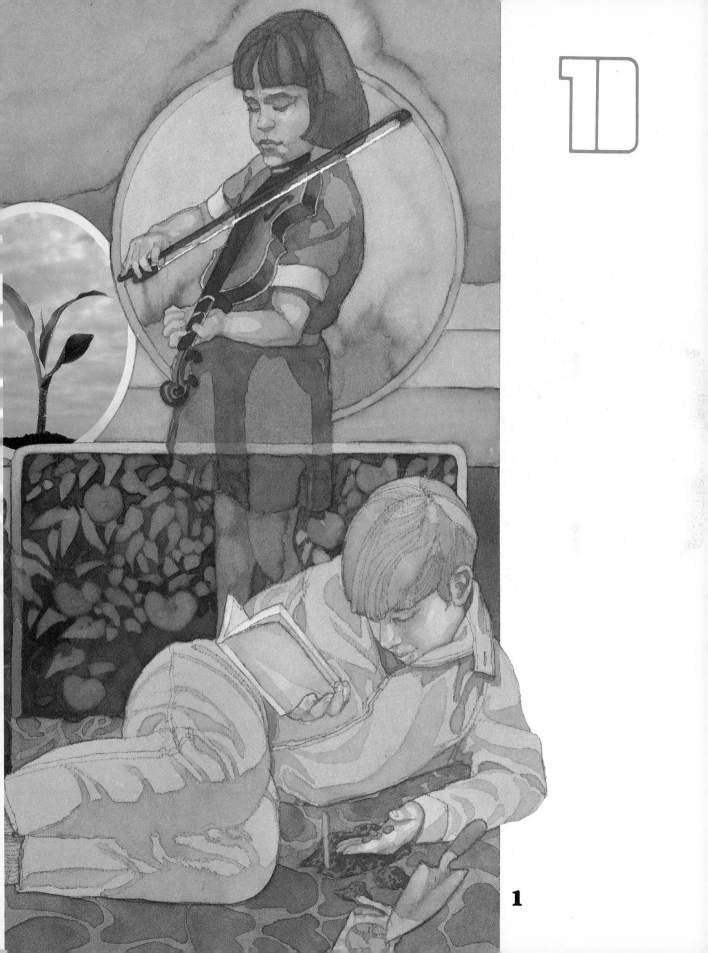

1

Overview:
The Writing Process

Writing has different steps.

Prewriting

Prewriting is the step in which you decide what you will write. You might make a list or talk to other people to discover ideas.

Writing

Writing a draft is the next step. Writing a draft means putting your words on paper. Your writing should tell about things in the order in which they happened.

Revising

Revising is the next step. Revising means reading your writing to find ways to make it better. Check to be sure your sentences are written correctly. Look for ways to make your writing clearer and more interesting.

Proofreading

In the proofreading step, you check your writing for errors. Check the spelling of your words. Check to see that you used punctuation correctly. Make sure your handwriting is clear.

Sharing

Sharing your writing with others can be fun. Other people can give you ideas to make your writing even better.

Thinking: Whole and Parts

STUDY

Lee is setting the table for dinner. Lee knows that a place setting is made of different **parts.** What are some parts of a place setting? These parts make up the **whole** place setting.

REMEMBER

A **whole** is made of different **parts.**

PRACTICE

Finding a Whole   Look at the parts shown in the picture on the left. Find the picture that shows the whole. Write *a, b,* or *c.*

WRITE

A List   Read page 276 of the **DATABANK.** Write a list of foods that make up a good breakfast. Try to choose a food from each of the four food groups. Title your list "Parts of a Good Breakfast."

4

Prewriting: Sentence Parts

Lisa goes to the grocery store.

Naming part   **Telling part**

Who is this sentence about?
What does the person in the
sentence do?

☑ A sentence has parts.

☑ The **naming part** names *who* or *what* the
  sentence is about.

☑ The **telling part** tells what the naming part
  does or *did*.

Matching Sentence Parts   Match each
naming part with a telling part. Then write each
complete sentence.

Naming Parts	Telling Parts
1. Bananas	a. fixed her own lunch.
2. The boys	b. grow in bunches.
3. Dan	c. ate their oranges.
4. Carmen	d. knows milk is good for him.

Sentence Parts   Write five sentence parts
about food. Your five sentence parts can be
naming parts or telling parts.

Writing: Sentences

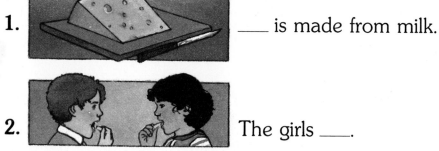

Tony sees these sentences in his book.
He must add a naming part or a telling part.
Each sentence must make sense.

1. _____ is made from milk.

2. The girls _____.

What would Tony add to complete sentence 1?

Is this word the naming part or the telling part of the sentence?

What could Tony add to complete sentence 2?

Are these words the naming part or the telling part of the sentence?

REMEMBER

☑ A sentence must have a **naming part** and a **telling part.**

☑ A sentence must make sense.

Finding Sentences   Read each group of words. Copy only the complete sentences.

1. Sue and Jamie
2. The apples are in the bowl.
3. Sue and Jamie are sitting at a table.
4. is in the glass.
⭐ 5. Jamie is eating an apple, and Sue is drinking milk.

Writing Sentences   Copy the sentences. Use words from the box to complete each sentence.

Meg   had water in it   The green beans were large and fresh   bought some green beans

6. Meg ___.
7. ___ were very fresh.
8. ___ put the beans in the pan.
9. The pan ___.
⭐ 10. The green beans ___.

Sentences   Write five complete sentences of your own. Use the sentence parts about food that you wrote on page 5. Add the missing sentence parts.

Revising: Sentences

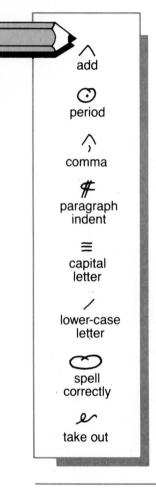

∧
add

⊙
period

⌄
comma

#
paragraph
indent

≡
capital
letter

/
lower-case
letter

⌒
spell
correctly

℮
take out

Ramón helped to plant a new garden. Here are some sentences he wrote about the garden.

> Mom and planted corn.
>
> Dad planted beets. Marsha planted beets.

Ramón reads his sentences quietly to himself. He notices that he has forgotten a word in the first sentence. He corrects the error using ∧ to show where the missing word belongs.

> Mom and ∧I planted corn.

Ramón improved the last two sentences by combining them. He joined together the two naming parts.

> Dad ∧and planted beets. Marsha planted beets.

◢ Read your sentences after you have finished writing them. Ask yourself these questions.
- Did I add any missing words?
- Did I use words that say clearly what I want them to?
- Are there any short sentences that can be combined?

Combining Sentences   Read the sentences.
Combine them into one sentence.

1. Dad planted some tulips. I planted some tulips.
2. Marsha mowed the grass. Mom mowed the grass.
3. Dad built a fence. I built a fence.
4. Marsha cut some roses. I cut some roses.
   ⋆ 5. Mom weeded. Dad weeded. Marsha weeded. I weeded.

Revising Sentences   Read each sentence. Find the missing word. Write each sentence correctly.

6. I like to pick berries at farm.
7. Dad and use a basket to hold the berries.
8. Fresh are very good to eat.
9. Dad takes a picture me picking berries.
   ⋆ 10. Like fresh berries on cereal.

Sentences   Look at the sentences you wrote
about food on page 7. Read each sentence quietly to yourself. Decide if it makes sense. Did you leave out any words from the naming part of the sentence? Did you leave out any words from the telling part? Did you forget to add any little words? Change anything you need to.

Proofreading: Sentences

STUDY

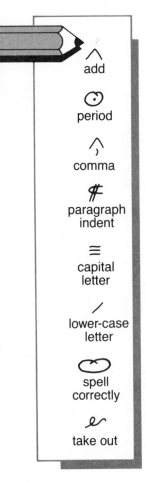

∧
add

⊙
period

∧
,
comma

#
paragraph
indent

≡
capital
letter

/
lower-case
letter

⌒
spell
correctly

ℓ
take out

Julia has written some sentences about her breakfast. When she reads her sentences, she finds some mistakes. Julia uses editing marks to show changes in the sentences she wrote.

> i ate cereal with milk and ̸Fruit
> for breakfast.
>
> piece
> I also ate a ⟨peice⟩ of toast⊙

She uses ≡ to show where a capital letter is needed. She uses / to show where a small letter is needed. She uses ⊙ to show where a period is needed.

Julia also checks her sentences for correct spelling. She circles each word that is spelled incorrectly. She writes the word correctly above the circle.

Here is another of Julia's edited sentences. What changes did she make?

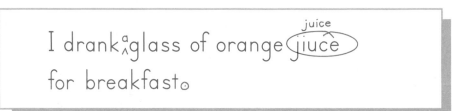

> a   juice
> I drank∧glass of orange ⟨jiuce⟩
> for breakfast⊙

✓ Proofread your work. Ask yourself these questions.

- Did I spell everything correctly?
- Did I use capital and small letters correctly?
- Did I punctuate sentences correctly?

Copying Sentences Correctly   Copy Julia's sentences. Make any changes that are shown by the editing marks Julia used.

Proofreading Sentences   Copy these sentences and correct them. Use editing marks.

1. Mom made fresh corn for dinner
2. my sister picked tomatoes in the garden.
3. Dad baked bred this morning.
4. We bought pears and apples at market.
★ 5. we all sat down to eat Healthy dinner

A Final Copy   Read the sentences about food that you revised on page 9. Is the first letter in each sentence a capital letter? Did you use capital letters and small letters correctly? Did you end each sentence with a period? Did you forget any words? Did you spell any words incorrectly? Correct your sentences if you need to.

Mechanics: Handwriting

STUDY

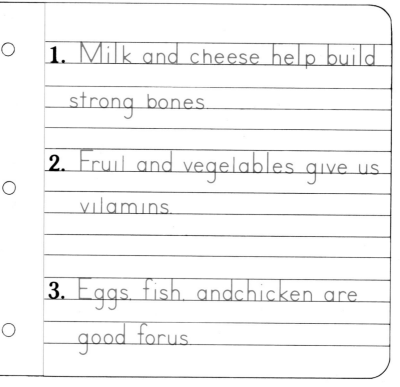

Mark has written three sentences. They tell about the kinds of foods that are healthy to eat. Here are his sentences.

1. Milk and cheese help build strong bones.

2. Fruit and vegetables give us vitamins.

3. Eggs, fish, and chicken are good for us.

Mark reads his sentences. He sees that his handwriting is not very good. Mark knows that even good sentences are hard to read if the handwriting is not clear. Mark decides to write his sentences again. He will use better handwriting.

Which letters or words in Mark's sentences are not written correctly? Use the handwriting chart on pages 262–263 of the **DATABANK**.

- ☑ Make sure your letters are written correctly.
- ☑ Remember to cross the letter *t* and to dot the letters *i* and *j*.
- ☑ Leave enough space between the words that you write.

Copying Sentences Neatly   Write Mark's sentences correctly. Use handwriting that is correct and clear.

Writing Sentences   Write these sentences. Use the handwriting chart on pages 262–263 of the **DATABANK** to check your letters.

1. I made lunch for my little brother today.
2. I fixed a tuna fish sandwich for him.
3. I poured a glass of milk for him to drink.
4. I also gave him an apple to eat.
5. My brother said he liked the lunch I made.

Sentences   Look at the sentences you proofread on page 11. Is your handwriting clear and easy to read? Is there anything you need to change?

Sharing Your Writing

Sometimes it is nice to write something for yourself alone. Most writing is fun to share with others. Sharing your ideas is an important part of writing.

When you share your writing, do not be afraid to listen to what others think. Other people can help you find ways to make your writing better.

Some people may want to share their writing with you. Remember that they probably worked hard on their writing. Make your suggestions to them in a kind and helpful way.

Here are some ways to share your writing.

Read Aloud   Read aloud your writing to a friend or to a group of people. Use your voice to make your writing sound interesting and exciting. Then discuss ways to improve your writing.

Act Out   Act out your writing as if it were a show. Discuss ways to improve the writing.

Make a Tape Recording   Record what you have written on a tape. Be sure it sounds interesting and lively. Play your recording to a friend or to a group of people.

Make a Class Book   Work with your class to put together a class book. The book should include a piece of writing from each child.

Start a Class Newspaper
Ask class members to write articles for a newspaper. Arrange the articles to look like pages in a newspaper.

Set Up a Bulletin Board   Have members of your class take turns showing their writing on a bulletin board.

Sharing Sentences   Think about each group of sentences described below. Discuss a good way for the writer to share the sentences.

PRACTICE

1. These sentences are about farm sounds.
2. These sentences are about baby animals.
3. These sentences are about your school.
4. These sentences are about your friends.
5. These sentences are about different jobs.

Sentences   Make a final copy of the sentences you wrote on page 13.

WRITE

Have a friend read aloud your sentences. Ask your friend if the sentences make sense.

SHARE

Prewrite   Choose a topic for your composition project. You may use one of the topics below or choose one of your own.

Write   Begin by putting your ideas on paper. Be sure to write using complete sentences.

Revise   Read your writing again and try to make it better. Check to be sure your sentences are written correctly. Also, look for ways to make your writing clearer and more interesting.

Proofread   Read your writing again. Proofread it for errors in spelling and punctuation. Also, check to be sure your handwriting is clear.

Share   Share your writing with others.

Music/Art

Look at the painting on page 297 of the **DATABANK**. Pretend you are this famous painting hanging in a museum. Write sentences telling about three different people who look at you.

Communications

Pretend you will read a morning greeting to all the children in your school. Write your greeting in three sentences. Then read the sentences to a friend. Ask your friend if the sentences are clear.

Literature

Write three sentences about a book so that people will want to read it. Tell about some of the people or animals in the story. Tell about some of the exciting things in the story.

Mathematics

Count the students in your classroom today. Next, count the desks in your classroom. Then write three sentences. The first sentence should tell how many students are present. The second sentence should tell how many desks there are. The third sentence should tell how many desks will not be used today.

Science

Write three sentences that tell what an animal looks like. Do not name the animal. Read your sentences to a friend. Ask your friend to guess the name of the animal.

Social Studies

Look up information about your state. Then write three sentences about your state. Write about your state flower or your state bird.

Statements

You speak and write in sentences. A **sentence** is a group of words that states a complete thought.

Read the sentence in color.

1. Maria plays the piano.

Who is the sentence about? What does Maria do? The sentence is about Maria. She plays the piano.

A sentence may be a statement. **Statements** tell something. Read this statement.

2. Mrs. Wilson gives piano lessons.

Who gives piano lessons? The statement tells the answer.

Notice that a statement begins with a capital letter. A statement ends with a **period** . .

Read the statements below. As you read, ask yourself these questions. Who comes to the classroom? What is the teacher doing?

3. Maria comes to the classroom.

4. The teacher is waiting.

- ☑ A **sentence** tells a complete thought.
- ☑ A **statement** tells something.
- ☑ A statement begins with a capital letter.
- ☑ A statement ends with a **period** . .

18

Finding Statements Read each group of words. Copy each statement.

1. Maria takes piano lessons.
2. Practices every day.
3. The teacher.
4. She waits for her lesson.
5. Maria will play a new song today.

Writing Statements Write each group of words in the correct order. Each group of words should make a statement.

6. early. is Maria
7. hard. works The girl very
8. sits She at the piano.
9. song The pretty. sounds
10. teacher The Maria. of is proud
11. children listen The carefully.
12. music. like They the
13. children The clapping. are
14. for She class. her plays
15. practices. day Every Maria

Sentences Draw a picture. Show a way that you would like to make music. Write three statements telling about the picture.

Questions

Some sentences ask something. These sentences are called **questions**. Read these questions.

1. Can you play the flute?

2. Do you like music?

Notice that each question asks something. What is your answer to each question?

A question begins with a capital letter. A question ends with a **question mark ?** .

Read these two questions. Notice the words in color.

3. Who is playing the flute?

4. Where is your music?

What words are at the beginning of each question? *Who* and *where* are often at the beginning of questions. The words *what, when, why,* and *how* may also be at the beginning of questions.

☑ A **question** asks something.

☑ A question begins with a capital letter.

☑ A question ends with a **question mark ?** .

☑ A question may begin with one of these words.

    Who   What   Where   Why   How   When

20

Finding Questions   Read the sentences. Copy each question.

1. The flute makes a pretty sound.
2. Can you play this song?
3. I want to hear it.
4. What time is your lesson?
5. When did you start to play?
6. Here is the new music.
7. Why are you late today?
8. Who is your music teacher?
9. Don't you like this song?
10. Which of these songs can you play?

Completing Questions   Copy and complete each question. Use each word only once.

Who	What	When	Where	Why

11. ___ is your favorite song?
12. ___ came to the lesson?
13. ___ is your flute?
14. ___ will your lesson begin?
15. ___ is your teacher happy?

A Poem   Write a rhyme made of a question and an answer. In the first line, ask a question. In the second line, write a statement that answers the question. Make the last word in the answer rhyme with the last word in the question.

Exclamations

Some sentences show strong feelings. These sentences are called **exclamations.**

Read these two sentences. Notice the words in color.

1. How lovely the music sounds!
2. What a beautiful song it is!

How does the music sound? What kind of song is it? The words *lovely* and *beautiful* tell about feelings. They help to make the sentences show strong feelings.

Notice that an exclamation begins with a capital letter. An exclamation ends with an **exclamation point !** .

Read these two sentences. As you read, ask yourself these questions. What is the drummer like? What is the music like?

3. What a wonderful drummer he is!
4. That is the best music I have ever heard!

- ☑ An **exclamation** shows strong feelings.
- ☑ An exclamation begins with a capital letter.
- ☑ An exclamation ends with an **exclamation point !** .

Finding Exclamations Read each sentence.
Copy each exclamation.

1. Ned is ready for his lesson.
2. Oh no, he lost his music!
3. Wow, you found it!
4. The lesson can begin.
 5. My music lesson was awful!

Writing Exclamations Write each group of
words in the correct order. Each group of words
should make an exclamation.

6. It so exciting! is
7. wonderful What song! a
8. that loud! is Wow,
9. great a What idea!
10. easy is How play! it to
11. late is! How my teacher
12. out, drum Watch falling! the is
13. toe! fell my it Ouch, on
 14. my Oh split! no, reed
 15. arrangement! an What unusual

Exclamations Pretend you took a pet mouse   WRITE
with you to your music lesson. What would
happen if it escaped? Draw a funny picture. Write
three exclamations to go with your picture.

Command

Some sentences tell someone to do something. These sentences are **commands.** Read these commands.

1. Show me your trumpet.

2. Play a song for us.

Notice that each sentence tells someone what to do.

Now read this command.

3. Please play a new song.

What word is at the beginning of the command? The word *please* is often used in a command. Notice that a command begins with a capital letter. A command ends with a period .

Read these commands. As you read, ask yourself this question. What is the person being asked to do?

4. Study the music.

5. Try again.

☑ A **command** tells someone to do something.

☑ A command begins with a capital letter.

☑ A command ends with a period . .

Finding Commands   Read each sentence.
Copy each command.

1. Come at three o'clock.
2. Please be on time today.
3. Did you practice today?
4. Here is a new song.
5. Please play the song again.
6. Do you like the trumpet?
7. Listen to this pretty song.
8. Find the right note.
9. Ask someone to help you.
10. Try to play it again.

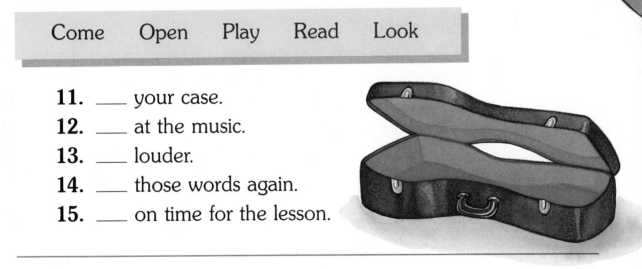

Completing Commands   Copy and complete
each sentence. Use each word from the box only
once.

| Come | Open | Play | Read | Look |

11. ___ your case.
12. ___ at the music.
13. ___ louder.
14. ___ those words again.
15. ___ on time for the lesson.

Directions   Write three sentences. Tell
someone what steps to follow when putting away
a trumpet. Write your directions as commands.

Capitalization and End Punctuation

There are four kinds of sentences.
Read these sentences.

1. The contest will begin soon.
2. Who will be the winner?
3. Please sit down.
4. Oh, the music is lovely!

Notice that every sentence begins with a capital letter. A **statement** tells something. Which sentence is a statement? A **question** asks something. Which sentence is a question?

A **command** tells someone to do something. Which sentence is a command? An **exclamation** shows strong feeling. Which sentence is an exclamation?

Notice that a statement and a command end with a period. What mark follows a question? What mark follows an exclamation?

- ✓ Every sentence begins with a capital letter.
- ✓ A statement and a command end with a period . .
- ✓ A question ends with a question mark ? .
- ✓ An exclamation ends with an exclamation point ! .

Finding Sentences   Copy each sentence that
is written correctly.

    1. who plays the violin

    2. Hooray, Lee was a winner!

    3. Please be on time.

    4. Where shall we sit?

    5. The contest begins tonight.

Writing Sentences   Write each
sentence correctly. Use a capital letter
and the correct end mark.

    6. we are going to the contest

    7. when does the contest begin

    8. please find me a seat

    9. you and I can sit here

    10. the musicians are on stage

    11. how excited they are

    12. wow, the singer is great

    13. are you enjoying the contest

★   **14.** tell me all about the performance

★   **15.** what a wonderful job the contestants
        are doing

Sentences   Imagine that you are playing an
instrument in a contest. Write four sentences
about the contest. Use one of each of the four
kinds of sentences.

Understanding Parts of a Sentence

STUDY

Every sentence has a naming part and a telling part. The naming part of the sentence names who or what the sentence is about. The naming part is called the **subject** of the sentence.

The telling part of the sentence tells what the subject does. The telling part is called the **predicate** of the sentence.

Read the sentence.

1. Kareem plays the drum.

Who is the sentence about? *Kareem* is the subject of the sentence. Read the sentence again. What does Kareem do? The words *plays the drum* are the predicate of the sentence.

Read the sentence below. As you read, ask yourself these questions. Who or what is the sentence about? What does the subject do?

2. Fred plays the tuba well.

REMEMBER

- ☑ The **subject** of a sentence names who or what the sentence is about.
- ☑ The **predicate** of a sentence tells what the subject does.

28

Finding the Subject and Predicate Copy each sentence. Draw one line under the subject. Draw two lines under the predicate.

1. The band will give a concert.
2. Alex practices every day.
3. Three children learn a new song.
4. Jack likes the soft music.
5. Ms. Denny teaches the band.
6. The teacher helps the children.
7. This band plays very well.
8. The music sounds beautiful.
   ⭐ 9. Parents and friends come to the concert.
   ⭐ 10. The audience claps enthusiastically.

Writing Sentences Choose a subject from the first box. Choose a predicate from the second box. Write the sentences you make.

The leader
The horns
The drummers
Friends
The concert

will begin soon.
tap the rhythm.
directs the band.
sound clear.
come to the concert.

A Poster Read the facts about musical instruments on page 296 of the **DATABANK.** Make a poster for a concert. Write three sentences about the concert. Draw one line under each subject. Draw two lines under each predicate.

Sound Words

STUDY

In our language some words stand for the sounds we hear. Writers use these sound words to help their readers hear what is going on. Some examples of sound words are *buzz, crash, hum,* and *thump.* When you say these words, can you hear the sounds?

PRACTICE

Matching Sound Words With Pictures

Look at the pictures. Choose the sound word in the Word Bank that matches each instrument. Write the words on a piece of paper.

| **Word Bank** | clang | toot | tweet |
| | boom | bong | oompah |

1.   2.   3.

4.   5.   ★ 6.

Writing Sentences   Pretend that you are one of the musical instruments above. Write three sentences describing the sound you make.

Language and Logic

True Sentences and False Sentences

Look at the picture. Is sentence 1 true or false?

1. There are three boys.

You see three boys in the picture. So sentence 1 is **true.**

Look at the picture again. Is sentence 2 true or false?

2. The horn is blue.

You see that the horn is not blue. So sentence 2 is not true. It is **false.**

Identifying True and False Sentences

Look at the picture again. Read each sentence below. If the sentence is true, write *true*. If the sentence is false, write *false*.

1. There are two girls.

2. There are two drums.

3. There is only one violin.

4. The flute player is a girl.

5. The drummer is wearing a green shirt.

6. All of the instruments have strings.

Conducting a Discussion: Listening and Speaking

Members of the craft club were talking about a cooking project. Read what they said.

Sara: I think we should make . . .

Jamie: Let's make muffins.

You should always take turns when speaking to someone. Did Jamie let Sara finish talking? What should he have done? It is important to speak slowly and clearly. You should look at the person to whom you are talking. Why is this a good idea?

To be a good listener, look at the speaker and pay attention. Ask questions if you do not understand something.

Read what Seth and Mary said.

Seth: Let's put dates in the muffins.

Mary: When should we put the dates in?

How did Mary use good manners? How else can you show good manners in a discussion?

✓ When having a discussion, take turns and speak clearly.

✓ Pay attention and ask questions.

Writing Rules Copy each sentence. Finish each one with the correct word or words.

1. A speaker should speak ___.
2. If you don't understand, ask ___.
3. A listener should look at the ___.
4. Take turns ___.
⭐ 5. When you speak, look at ___.

Applying Rules Complete each sentence. Use the answers from the box.

> take turns talking   pay attention
> speak clearly   look at   ask a question

6. Pam and Al discuss how to stir the batter. They should ___.
7. Ingrid tells Uli how she bakes at home. Uli should ___ Ingrid.
8. Uli does not understand something Ingrid says. Uli should ___.
9. Tina talks fast, and Jimi cannot understand. Tina needs to ___.
⭐ 10. Alva tells Inez her idea for sharing the muffins. Inez should look at Alva and ___.

A Poster Make a poster to show one of the important listening or speaking rules. Write the rule. Draw one picture showing what to do and one picture showing what *not* to do.

Listening to and Following Directions

Mr. Robinson is giving the class directions for making a picture with mosaic tiles.

Directions explain how to make or do something. How can the students be good listeners?

When you listen to directions, you should listen to all the directions first and picture each step. Should the students start to work as soon as Mr. Robinson starts to speak? What should they do as they listen?

When you follow directions, do all the steps in the correct order. Do not leave out any steps. What might happen if the students mix up the steps?

Mario does not know what a mosaic is. How can he find out?

- ◪ **Directions** explain how to make or do something.
- ◪ Listen to all the directions.
- ◪ Picture each step.
- ◪ Do all the steps in order.

Following Oral Directions   Your teacher will give you directions for drawing some pictures using shapes. Listen to and follow the directions.

Writing Directions   On a sheet of paper, write directions for making a sailboat using only a triangle, a rectangle, and a circle. Pass the paper to a partner. See if your partner can follow your directions.

A List of Directions   Listen to your teacher read directions for making a mosaic. Ask questions if you need to. You may ask how to spell something or you may ask what a word means. You may ask your teacher to repeat something, too. Then write a list of all the steps.

Talking on the Telephone

Mr. Robinson called to speak to Betsy's mother. Betsy answered the telephone. Read their conversation.

Betsy:	Hello.
Mr. Robinson:	Hello. This is Mr. Robinson. Is your mother at home?
Betsy:	Yes. Please wait a moment. I will get her.
Mr. Robinson:	Thank you.

You speak and listen when you use the telephone. When you call someone, be polite and give your name. Be helpful and speak clearly when you answer the telephone. Did Betsy and Mr. Robinson follow these rules? What polite words did they use?

- ✓ Be polite and helpful on the telephone.
- ✓ Give your name.
- ✓ Speak clearly.

Using Telephone Skills   Complete the telephone conversation. Use words from the box.

This is Leah.	Hello.	please
This is Joel.	Thank you.	

Leah: ___
Joel: Hello. ___ May I speak to Leah, ___?
Leah: ___
Joel: May I borrow your hammer and saw?
Leah: Yes, you may.
Joel: ___ I will come to get them.

Using Polite Words   Copy the telephone conversation. Replace the underlined words with polite words.

Lana: <u>What do you want?</u>
Rafe: Hello. <u>Is Lana around?</u>
Lana: <u>Who wants to know?</u>
Rafe: Would you like to come to our woodworking club today?
Lana: <u>Why should I?</u>
Rafe: <u>Okay. I'll hang up now.</u>

Woodworking Club

A Script   Imagine that you are calling a friend. You want your friend to help you with a woodworking project. Write a script to tell what each of you would say. Follow the rules for polite speaking. Share your script with the class.

Making Introductions

Mike Brown wanted to **introduce** his friend Andy to his mother. He spoke slowly and clearly. Read what he said.

Mike: Mother, this is my friend Andy. Andy is showing our craft club how to weave.

You should say the older person's name first in an introduction. Did Mike do this? You should tell something about the person you are introducing. What did Mike tell about Andy? Why is this a good idea?

Read what Mrs. Brown and Andy said.

Mrs. Brown: Hello, Andy.

Andy: How do you do, Mrs. Brown?

What polite words did Mrs. Brown and Andy say?

- ✓ When you **introduce** people, say the older person's name first.
- ✓ Give some facts about the person you introduce.
- ✓ Use polite words.
- ✓ Stand straight and speak slowly and clearly.

38

Making Introductions   Read each
introduction. Write the better one from each pair.

    1. Dino, this is Mrs. Houston.
        Mrs. Houston, this is my friend Dino. He
        is interested in helping us weave our rug.
    2. Uncle Chu, this is Dot. She is a weaver.
        Uncle Chu, this girl is a weaver.
    3. Mom, meet Rosita.
        Mom, this is my new friend Rosita. She
        wove a rug all by herself.

Acting Out Introductions   Work in teams of
three students. Act out these introductions.

    4. Mary introduces William to her
        father. Mary and William have
        woven a wall-hanging together.
    5. Gina introduces Fred to Ms. Angelo.
        Ms. Angelo is a weaver. The children
        have been working in craft club on a
        weaving project.

An Introduction   Imagine that you are
introducing three adult weavers to your teacher.
Make up names for the weavers. Write something
that you could say about each weaver. Read
pages 270–272 in the **DATABANK** for ideas about
how weavers work.

Composition Write three sentences that tell about something that you like to do.

Grammar, Mechanics, and Usage Choose the example that is a complete sentence.

1. (a) This is coat. (b) This is my.
   (c) This is my coat. (d) Is my coat.

2. (a) Sue draws a picture. (b) Sue a picture.
   (c) Draws a picture. (d) Sue picture.

3. (a) The people the (b) The people are at work.
   (c) The people. (d) Are at work.

Choose the kind of sentence that is shown in each example.

4. Will Jack go? 5. Dan is my friend.
   (a) statement (a) statement
   (b) question (b) exclamation

6. What a lovely picture! 7. Please stand up.
   (a) statement (a) exclamation
   (b) exclamation (b) command

Choose the correct way to write each sentence.

8. (a) She is my friend (b) she is my friend.
   (c) she is my friend. (d) She is my friend.

9. (a) The bird is flying. (b) the bird is flying.
   (c) The bird is flying (d) the bird is flying

Choose the correct way to write each sentence.

10. (a) May I help you.   (b) May I help you?
    (c) may I help you?   (d) May I help you!

11. (a) Please come here?   (b) please come here.
    (c) please come here!   (d) Please come here.

12. (a) What a beautiful hat!   (b) What a beautiful hat?
    (c) what a beautiful hat? (d) What a beautiful hat.

Choose whether the underlined sentence part is a
subject or a predicate.

13. Kelley <u>went to school.</u>   14. The boys <u>sing songs.</u>

    (a) subject (b) predicate   (a) subject (b) predicate

15. <u>The dog</u> ran fast.   16. Mike <u>likes oranges.</u>

    (a) subject (b) predicate   (a) subject (b) predicate

Practical Language Skills Chose a rule for speaking.

17. (a) Put words in ABC order. (b) Speak clearly.
    (c) Speak in a whisper.   (d) Look at the floor.

Choose a rule for listening.

18. (a) Use polite words.   (b) Look at the speaker.
    (c) Talk to a friend.   (d) Take turns speaking.

Choose the polite word or words in each sentence.

19. <u>Wait</u> a <u>moment</u>, <u>please</u>. 20. <u>Good-by</u>, <u>Dr.</u> <u>Green</u>.
   (a)   (b)   (c)   (a)   (b) (c)

Composition:
The Sentence

MESSAGES

Categorizing
Writing a Message
Revising and Proofreading
 a Message
Capitalization and Punctuation
Projects

Grammar, Mechanics,
and Usage: Nouns

AROUND THE COUNTRY

Nouns That Name People, Places, and Things
Proper Nouns
Capitalization of Names, Titles, and Place Names
Language History: Words From Different Parts of the Country
Language and Logic: *All* and *None* Sentences

Practical Language Skills:
Dictionary Skills

IN THE ART CLASS

ABC Order
Dictionary Guide Words
Dictionary Entries

Thinking: Categorizing

STUDY

Jill and her family are moving into a new house. They must tell the movers where to put each thing. Which of these belongs in the kitchen? Why?

REMEMBER

☑ Things can be put into groups.

☑ Things in a group are alike in some important way.

PRACTICE

Grouping Things Write these place names: *bedroom, living room, garage.* Then list the following things in the room in which they would belong. Some things may go in more than one room.

rake	dresser	couch
bed	shovel	tool box
television	table	toy box
lamp	alarm clock	night light
bicycle	bookcase	lawn mower

WRITE

A List Pretend that you are moving. Make a list of five things that might go in your bedroom.

Prewriting: A Message

Melinda wants to play at a friend's house. She does not want her father to worry. She thinks about what he needs to know. Then she will write him a **message**.

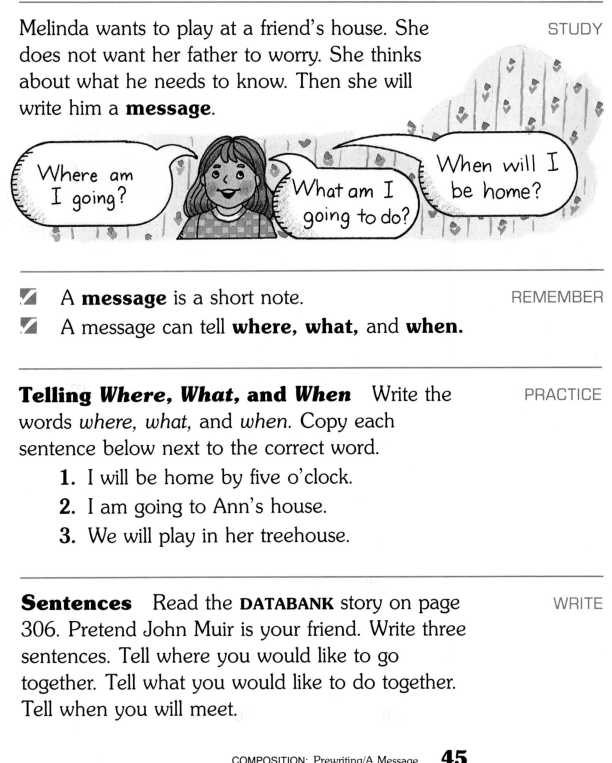

Where am I going?

What am I going to do?

When will I be home?

- ✓ A **message** is a short note.
- ✓ A message can tell **where, what,** and **when.**

Telling *Where, What, and When* Write the words *where, what,* and *when.* Copy each sentence below next to the correct word.

1. I will be home by five o'clock.
2. I am going to Ann's house.
3. We will play in her treehouse.

Sentences Read the **DATABANK** story on page 306. Pretend John Muir is your friend. Write three sentences. Tell where you would like to go together. Tell what you would like to do together. Tell when you will meet.

Writing: A Message

Tom answers the phone. The call is for his brother. But Larry is not home. Tom listens carefully so that he can write down the message. Tom writes this message to his brother.

Larry has a baseball game on May 5. The team will meet in the park at nine o'clock.

May 1, 1988

To Larry   From Tom

Jack called. You have a baseball game on May 5. The team will meet in the park at nine o'clock.

Who will get this message? Who took the message? What is the message?

☑ Tell whom the message is for.
☑ Tell who took the message.
☑ Put the important facts in the message.

Putting a Message in Order   Write a
message using these parts.

Linda called.
September 21, 1988
To Barb
You have a scout meeting on September 25.
The meeting is at Linda's house after school.
From Sam

Writing a Message   Write a message using
Melinda's facts from page 45. The message is
from Melinda to Dad. Use today's date in your
message.

A Message   Write a message to John Muir. Use
the sentences you wrote on page 45. Use today's
date in your message.

Revising: A Message

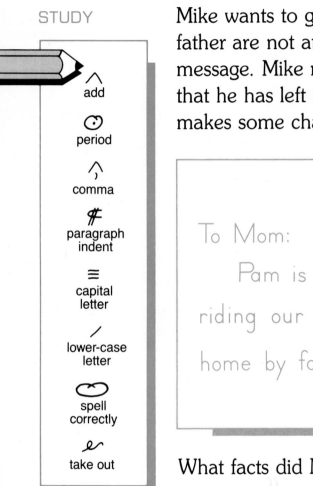

∧
add

⊙
period

∧̣
comma

#
paragraph
indent

≡
capital
letter

/
lower-case
letter

spell
correctly

take out

Mike wants to go to the library. His mother and father are not at home. He decides to write a message. Mike reads his message again. He finds that he has left out some important facts. He makes some changes in his message.

october 27, 1988

To Mom:

Pam is out. i am out. we are riding our bicycles. We will be home by four o'clock.

What facts did Mike add to his message?

Read each message that you write. Ask yourself these questions.

- Does my message have all the important facts?
- Does it tell whom the message is for and whom it is from?
- Does it tell when, where, and what?

• Are there short sentences I can combine?

Combining Sentences   Combine each pair of
sentences into a longer sentence.

PRACTICE

1. Rita sings at school.
   Aaron sings at school.
2. Nilda plays the guitar.
   Nilda plays the drums.
3. Frank practices the piano.
   Sally practices the piano.
4. Francie wrote some songs.
   Francie sang some songs.
5. Marcia has studied the violin.
   Kim has studied the violin.

Revising a Message   Read this message from
Mike to Pam. Write the message. Add facts that are
missing. Combine short sentences where you can.

From Mike

Beth called. Ricky called. You have band
practice on Friday afternoon.

A Revised Message   Read the message you
wrote to John Muir. Check to see if all the
important facts are there. Add any missing facts.

WRITE

Proofreading: A Message

STUDY

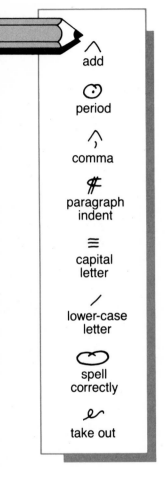

∧
add

⊙
period

∧
comma

#
paragraph
indent

≡
capital
letter

/
lower-case
letter

⌒
spell
correctly

ℓ
take out

Mike takes another look at his message. He finds that there are still a few mistakes to fix.

He remembers that the first letter of a month and the word *I* are always capital letters. He also remembers that a comma comes between the day and the year in a date.

He uses editing marks to show these changes. The mark ≡ shows where a capital letter is needed. The mark ∧ shows where a comma belongs. Here is Mike's edited message. What changes does he make?

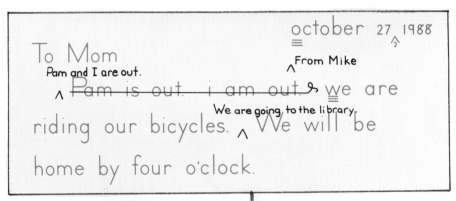

october 27, 1988

To Mom   From Mike

Pam and I are out.
Pam is out. i am out. we are
                    We are going to the library.
riding our bicycles. We will be

home by four o'clock.

50

✓ Proofread your work. Ask yourself these questions.

- Did I begin the months of the year with capital letters?
- Did I write the word *I* as a capital letter?
- Did I put a comma between the day and the year in a date?

REMEMBER

Proofreading a Message   Correct this message. Use capital letters and a comma where they are needed.

PRACTICE

                     December 14 1988
To Mom   From Jamie
Mrs. Hill called. The wool will be ready
on december 29. She said i could pick it
up at her house that morning.

A Final Copy   Read the message you revised on page 49. Did you use capital letters correctly? Did you remember to put a comma between the day and the year? Make a final copy of your message to John Muir.

WRITE

Share your message with your classmates. Ask them if all the important facts are there.

SHARE

Prewrite   Choose a topic for your composition project. You may use one of the topics below or choose one of your own.

Write   Think about what you want to say and write your message. Be sure your message tells the date, whom the message is for, whom it is from, and all the important facts.

Revise   Read your message again and try to make it better. Combine sentences if you can. Check to be sure your message tells what, where, and when.

Proofread   Read your message again. Proofread it for mistakes in spelling and punctuation. Be sure you used capital letters correctly.

Share   Make a final copy. Share your writing with others.

Literature
Read the story on pages 266–268 of the **DATABANK.** Pretend that you are a character in the story. Write a message to another character in the same story.

Crafts

Write a message to a parent. Explain that you are staying after school for cooking club. Be sure to tell how and when you will get home.

Health/Physical Education

Write a message to a parent. Explain that Mr. Jones called. He said that the new exercise class will begin next week. Use dates in your message.

Mathematics

Write a message to a friend. Ask your friend to meet you at a movie theater. Tell what time your friend should meet you. Tell what time the movie will end.

Science

Pretend you found a bottle at the beach. Write a message to put in the bottle. Tell someone who lives far away where and when you found the bottle.

Social Studies

Write a message to the children in your neighborhood about a story hour in the library. Tell the date and time of the story hour.

Nouns That Name People

STUDY

Most sentences have nouns. **Nouns** are words that name people, places, or things. Many nouns name people. Read these two sentences. Notice the words in color.

1. The girl packed yesterday.
2. Her father carried the suitcase.

Who packed yesterday? Who carried the suitcase? The words *girl* and *father* are nouns. Each of these nouns names a person.

Now read the sentences below. Look for the nouns that name people. As you read, ask yourself these questions. Who will pack the car? Who is going to New Mexico?

3. Her brother will pack the car.
4. The children are going to New Mexico.

REMEMBER

- Most sentences have nouns.
- Many nouns name people.

PRACTICE

Finding Nouns   Copy these sentences. Draw a line under the nouns that name people.

1. The driver stops the cab.
2. A man opens the door.

3. The twins go into the airport.
4. The clerk looks at their tickets.
5. A woman shows them the right gate.
6. The men sit by the door.
7. A teacher sits next to them.
8. A worker brings them lunch.
★ 9. The pilot talks to the forecaster about the weather.
★ 10. Grandmother meets the children at the Taos airport.

Writing Nouns   Copy and complete each sentence. Use each noun from the box only once.

| grandfather | relatives | niece | officer | cousin |

11. Their ___ waits in the car.
12. The ___ showed him where to park.
13. The girl waves to her little ___.
14. Aunt Ines gives her ___ a big hug.
15. Grandmother asks all the ___ to a big picnic.

Sentences   Imagine that you and your parents are at the airport. You are waiting for a relative. Write three sentences telling about some of the people who work at the airport. Use a noun that names a person in each sentence. Read pages 302–303 of the **DATABANK.** It gives facts about airports and the people who work in them.

WRITE

Nouns That Name Places

STUDY

Some nouns name **places.** These nouns tell where someone or something is. These nouns also tell where something happens. Read these two sentences. Notice the words in color.

1. Karen lives on a farm.
2. The fields are filled with horses.

Where does Karen live? What is filled with horses? The words *farm* and *fields* are nouns. Each of these nouns names a place.

Now read the sentences below. Look for the nouns that name places. As you read, ask yourself these questions. Where does Karen take the horses? Where are there many riding trails?

3. Karen takes the horses to the barn.
4. The hill has many riding trails.

REMEMBER

- Most sentences have nouns.
- Some nouns name places.

PRACTICE

Finding Nouns Copy these sentences. Draw a line under the nouns that name places.

1. Karen lives in an old house.
2. Her room has many pictures of horses.
3. She looks out on the woods.

56

4. Karen trains her horse in the ring.
5. Her family lives far from the city.
6. Karen and her dad go to the village.
7. He buys gas at the garage.
8. They stop at the store to buy hay.
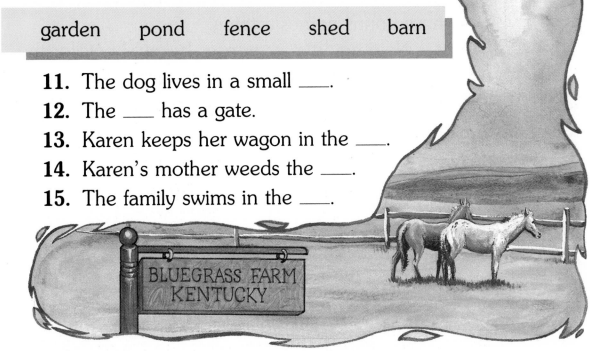 9. Dad leaves the truck in the lot beside the station.
10. They stop for lunch at a restaurant next to the post office.

Writing Nouns   Copy and complete each sentence. Use each noun from the box only once.

| garden | pond | fence | shed | barn |

11. The dog lives in a small ___.
12. The ___ has a gate.
13. Karen keeps her wagon in the ___.
14. Karen's mother weeds the ___.
15. The family swims in the ___.

BLUEGRASS FARM
KENTUCKY

A Map   Draw a map showing some places in your neighborhood. Choose places where you like to spend time. Under your map write three sentences about these places. Use a noun that names a place in each sentence.

WRITE

Nouns That Name Things

Some nouns name **things.** A tree is a thing. Words such as *cat, dog,* or *lions* are also nouns that name things. Read these two sentences. Notice the words in color.

1. Larry has peanuts.
2. The elephant is hungry.

What does Larry have? Who is hungry? The words *peanuts* and *elephant* are nouns. Each of these nouns names a thing.

Now read the sentences below. Look for the nouns that name things. As you read, ask yourself these questions. What is Larry waiting for? What does he give to the driver?

3. Larry waits for the tram.
4. He gives the money to the driver.

☑ Most sentences have nouns.

☑ Some nouns name things.

58

Finding Nouns   Copy these sentences. Draw a line under the nouns that name things.

1. Larry comes to the zoo by car.
2. He and his mother go through the gate.
3. The monkeys are chattering.
4. They hang by their tails.
5. The keeper feeds them fruit.
6. Larry walks over to see the tigers.
7. Their stripes make them hard to see.
8. They seem to disappear in the grass.
9. Larry buys film for his camera.
10. He takes pictures of many animals.

Writing Nouns   Copy and complete each sentence. Use each noun from the box only once.

| ticket | seat | camel | rope | ladder |

11. Larry wants to ride a ___.
12. He buys a ___ for the ride.
13. Larry climbs up a little ___.
14. The ___ is far from the ground.
15. Larry holds a thick ___.

A Poster   Make a zoo poster showing things you might see in a zoo. At the bottom write three sentences about these things. Use a noun that names a thing in each sentence.

Proper Nouns

Some nouns are special. A person has a special name. Streets, cities, and states have special names. Most pets have special names, too. Read these three sentences. Notice the words in color.

1. Rita Brown is a good friend.
2. She lives in Georgia.
3. Her cat is named Peaches.

What is the friend's name? Where does she live? What is her cat's name? *Rita Brown, Georgia,* and *Peaches* are all special names for a person, a state, and a pet. Notice that these special nouns begin with capital letters. Some special nouns have more than one word.

Now read the sentences below. As you read, ask yourself this question. Which noun names a special person, place, or thing?

4. My family went to Peachtree Plaza.
5. Mike walked in Central City Park.

REMEMBER

✔ Some nouns name special people, places, or things.

✔ These special nouns begin with capital letters.

✔ Some special nouns have more than one word.

60

Finding Nouns Copy these sentences. Draw a line under the nouns that name special people, places, or things.

1. My cousins live in Athens.
2. My aunt teaches at Augusta College.
3. Lisa Green is my oldest cousin.
4. She works in the Georgia Museum of Art.
5. Lisa lives in a house on Hill Street.
6. My cousin Bill goes to Park School.
7. Tom Johnson and Herb Lewis are his best friends.
8. Last year the boys went to the Farmers' Festival in Cordele.

Writing Nouns Copy and complete each sentence. Use each special noun from the box only once.

Stone Mountain	Tybee Lighthouse
Clark Lake	Lisa Green

9. ___ took a camping vacation.
10. She hiked up ___.
11. She swam in ___.
12. Lisa climbed the stairs of the ___.

A Postcard Write a postcard to a friend. Tell about things that you saw on a trip. Use a special noun in each sentence of your message.

Capitalization of Nouns

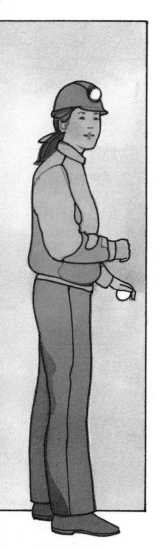

You know that some nouns are special. Special nouns include names of people, their titles, and their initials. Other special nouns name places such as states, cities, streets, buildings, parks, and rivers. Read these sentences. Notice the words in color.

1. Mr. Peter T. Ross went to Idaho.
2. He visited the Silver Dollar Mine.
3. The mine is near the Salmon River.

In what two ways are all of the words in color alike? All of these words are special nouns. All of these nouns begin with capital letters.

Now read these sentences. Why are certain words in each sentence written with capital letters?

4. Our guide was Dr. J. D. Peterson.
5. We met her outside the Taylor Building.
6. She lives near Moscow, Idaho.

What nouns name special places? What noun names a person? What title and initials does this person use?

✓ Begin names, titles, and initials with capital letters.

✓ Begin special place names with capital letters.

Capitalizing Nouns Write each noun correctly.

1. rocky mountains
2. silver city
3. snake river
4. mrs. landis
5. p. j. fisher
6. taylor creek
7. spirit lake
8. mr. bill bates
9. chief joseph
10. kellogg, idaho

Detail E.S. Paxon, "Lewis and Clark at Three Forks" Courtesy of the Montana Historical Society

Writing Proper Nouns Write this paragraph.
Use capital letters where they are needed.

In 1805, two explorers visited what is now idaho. They were m. lewis and william clark. The men were led by sacajawea, an Indian woman. The group used horses to cross the bitterroot mountains. They built boats and floated down the columbia river. The town of lewiston in idaho is named for mr. lewis.

A Journal Entry Pretend you are traveling west with Lewis and Clark. What new sights might you see? What adventures might you have? Write several sentences telling about an exciting day. Use a special noun in each sentence.

Language History

What Do You Call It?

STUDY

Sometimes people in different parts of the country use different words to mean the same thing. For example, people in some parts of the country call a large sandwich a *hero.* In other parts of the country, the same sandwich is called a *grinder,* a *hoagie,* or a *sub.* What is it called where you live?

PRACTICE

Choosing Words That Describe   Write a word to describe each picture.

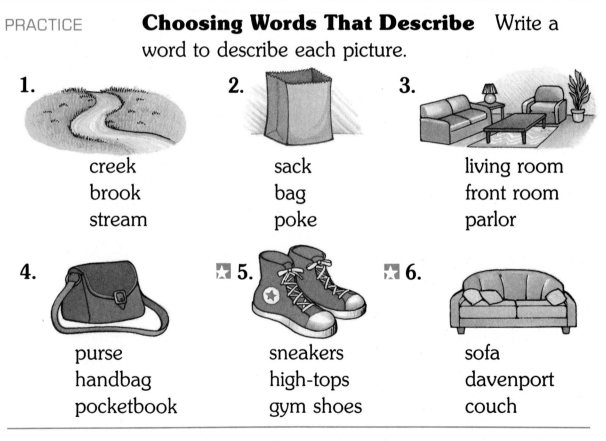

1.

creek
brook
stream

2.

sack
bag
poke

3.

living room
front room
parlor

4.

purse
handbag
pocketbook

⭐ 5.

sneakers
high-tops
gym shoes

⭐ 6.

sofa
davenport
couch

WRITE

Drawing a Cartoon   Draw your own cartoon showing what happens when two people use different words to mean the same thing.

Language and Logic

True-or-False Sentences

You know that some sentences are true. Some sentences are false. Read sentences 1 and 2.

1. Atlanta is the capital of Georgia.
2. Miami is the capital of Idaho.

Sentences 1 and 2 are statements. A statement tells you something or gives information. A statement may be true, or it may be false. Which sentence, 1 or 2, is true? Now read sentences 3 and 4.

3. What is the capital of Kentucky?
4. Drive to Santa Fe.

Sentence 3 is a question. Questions are neither true nor false. Sentence 4 is a command. Commands are neither true nor false.

Only statements can be true or false. Questions and commands are neither true nor false.

Identifying True-or-False Sentences

Read these sentences. Copy the ones that must be either true or false.

1. Do you live in Idaho?
2. Janet Lane lives in Idaho.
3. We visited Kentucky last month.
4. Show me your pictures.
5. Houston is in Texas.

 6. There are no cities in Texas.

ABC Order

ABC order is the order of the letters in the alphabet. You can put words in ABC order by looking at the first letter of each word. Put words that start with *a* first. Next put words that start with *b,* then *c,* then *d,* and so on.

Study these lists of words in ABC order.

1. artist   blue   coat   dry

2. air   cut   painter   star

Where does a word that starts with *a* belong? Does a word that starts with *c* come before or after one that starts with *p?*

You may have two words that start with the same letter. Look at the second letters to put the words in ABC order. Look at the letters in color in this list to see how to do this.

3. above   amount   answer   art

What letter begins each word? Are the letters in color in ABC order?

- ✓ **ABC order** is the order of letters in the alphabet.
- ✓ Use the first letter to put words in ABC order.
- ✓ Use the second letter if the first letters are the same.

Identifying ABC Order Write *Yes* if the
words are in ABC order. Write *No* if they are not.

1. animal   candle   box
2. brown   drawing   copper
3. doll   fan   light
4. map   paste   wall
5. hurry   letter   eye
6. fair   foot   melt
7. chalk   nose   name
8. game   school   sleep
★ 9. rain   ready   run
★ 10. green   gasp   gold

Putting Words in ABC Order
Write each list in ABC order.

11. brush   easel   art
12. water   red   marker
13. draw   picture   paper
★ 14. crayon   clean   color
★ 15. pen   purple   paint

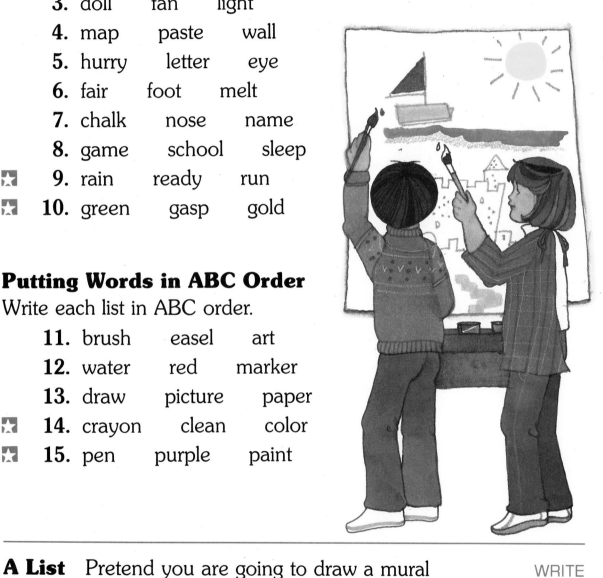

A List Pretend you are going to draw a mural
about the beach. Make a list of ten things you
could draw. Write the words in ABC order. For
facts about the beach, see pages 298–299 in the
DATABANK.

Dictionary Guide Words

A **dictionary** is a book that lists words and their meanings. The words in a dictionary are in ABC order. **Guide words** at the top of each page help you find words quickly. The first guide word is the first word on the page. The second guide word is the last word on the page. Look at these guide words.

1. **button/card**
2. **rock/string**

Button is the first word on the first page. What is the last word? What is the first word on the second page?

Words that come between the guide words are in ABC order. Look at these guide words. The words in color also appear on the page.

3. **march/net**   miss   monkey   music

The words *miss, monkey,* and *music* all come after *march* in ABC order. They all come before *net.* Would the word *muffin* be on this page? Would the word *note* be on this page?

- **Guide words** show the first and last words on a dictionary page.
- Words that come between the guide words are in ABC order.

68

Using Guide Words   Write the word or words
that come between each set of guide words.

    1. **bat/coat**   always   bring   dust

    2. **new/orange**   night   top   pop

    3. **gray/happy**   girl   gust   table

⭐   4. **dark/dust**   deep   done   dye

⭐   5. **tent/trust**   talk   there   turtle

Matching Guide Words   Copy the sets of
guide words. Write each word from the box next
to the guide words that show where it would be
found in the dictionary.

| thread | string | hanger | cut | bean |
| spool | turn | hook | dangle | blue |

    6. **bad/comb**

    7. **crab/dry**

    8. **green/hunt**

    9. **set/tale**

⭐ 10. **tear/twist**

A List of Guide Words   Write five things you
could hang on a mobile. Find each word in your
dictionary. Write the guide words for each page.

Dictionary Entries

The words in dark type on a dictionary page are called **entry words.** An entry word and all the information the dictionary gives about it are the **entry.** A dictionary entry tells the meaning of a word. Look at this example.

> **clay** (klā), a sticky kind of earth.

What is the entry word? What does it mean?
    Some entry words mean more than one thing.

> **hard** (hard), **1** not soft. **2** not easy.

Numbers show the different meanings. You can use sentence clues to find which meaning you want to use. Read these sentences.

1. The dry clay was very hard.

2. The test was too hard.

Which meaning of *hard* is used in each sentence? How can you tell?

☑ A dictionary tells what **entry words** mean.

☑ If an entry word has more than one meaning, use sentence clues to find which meaning you want.

Finding Definitions   Look up each underlined
word in a dictionary. Answer each question.
1. Can <u>beautiful</u> mean "pretty"?
2. What is another word for <u>kiln</u>?
3. What can you put in a <u>vase</u>?
4. What is another word for <u>crock</u>?
5. Can you make a <u>statue</u> from stone?

Choosing the Correct Definition   Look up
each underlined word. Write the correct meaning.
6. He made a <u>model</u> of a horse in art class.
7. You can <u>form</u> clay into many things.
8. Sara made a <u>set</u> of plates.
9. Turn on the oven <u>fire</u> to bake the cups.
10. Sandy painted a jar <u>orange</u>.
11. Andrew made a <u>dish</u> out of clay.
12. You can <u>roll</u> clay into a long snake.
13. <u>Squeeze</u> the clay in your hand.
14. Now <u>scratch</u> a picture in the clay.
15. We used a potter's <u>wheel</u> in class.

Sentences   Look up each word below in a
dictionary. Choose one meaning of each word.
Use the word in a sentence.

smooth   marble   design   palette   bowl

Composition Write a message to a parent. Explain that you are staying after school. You will be helping the drama club make costumes for a play.

Grammar, Mechanics, and Usage Choose the date that is written correctly.

1. ⓐ may 2 1988   ⓑ May 2 1988
   ⓒ may 2, 1988   ⓓ May 2, 1988
2. ⓐ december 1, 1988   ⓑ december 1 1988
   ⓒ December 1, 1988   ⓓ December 1 1988

Choose the word that tells about each underlined noun.

3. The <u>library</u> is near here.
   ⓐ person   ⓑ place
   ⓒ thing
4. My <u>teacher</u> is nice.
   ⓐ person   ⓑ place
   ⓒ thing
5. This <u>tree</u> is very tall.
   ⓐ person   ⓑ place
   ⓒ thing
6. The <u>farmer</u> has two cows.
   ⓐ person   ⓑ place
   ⓒ thing

Choose the correct way to write each special noun.

7. ⓐ Sue parker   ⓑ Sue Parker
8. ⓐ Mr. Greg Jones   ⓑ Mr. Greg jones
9. ⓐ R. J. Martin   ⓑ r. j. Martin
10. ⓐ lima, Ohio   ⓑ Lima, Ohio
11. ⓐ Tampa, Florida   ⓑ tampa, florida

Practical Language Skills Choose the words that are written in ABC order.

12. (a) car   look   frog   (b) look   frog   car
    (c) frog   car   look   (d) car   frog   look
13. (a) draw   girl   here   (b) girl   draw   here
    (c) here   girl   draw   (d) draw   here   girl
14. (a) pail   pour   pink   (b) pail   pink   pour
    (c) pour   pink   pail   (d) pink   pour   pail

Choose the word that would be on the same page as each pair of guide words.

15. prize/quite
    (a) peg   (b) puff
    (c) rain

16. kitten/leg
    (a) keep   (b) long
    (c) last

17. swim/team
    (a) tail   (b) tool
    (c) ship

18. fresh/gentle
    (a) girl   (b) far
    (c) gate

Choose the best ending for each sentence.

19. An entry word is ___
    (a) a word that has
        only one meaning.
    (c) a word in red on a
        dictionary page.
    (b) a word at the top of
        a dictionary page.
    (d) a word in dark type
        on a dictionary page.

20. Entry words are ___
    (a) always in red.
    (c) always in ABC order.
    (b) always numbered.
    (d) not in a dictionary.

Matching Sentence Parts (pages 5–7)

Match each naming part with a telling part. Then write each complete sentence.

Naming Parts	Telling Parts
1. My dog	a. tastes good.
2. The children	b. barks a lot.
3. This tree	c. are sleeping.
4. Cindy	d. paints a picture.
5. This orange	e. has many leaves.

Completing Sentences (pages 6–7)

Use the words in the box to complete the sentences. Write the sentences that you make.

a. The boys	b. washed the dishes.
c. sang in the tree.	d. The car

6. ___ played in the park.   7. Mary Ann ___

8. The bird ___   9. ___ will not start.

Statements, Questions, Exclamations, and Commands

Copy the sentences that are written correctly. (pages 18–27)

10. Where is bill   11. What a beautiful day!

12. She is my friend.   13. Please sit down.

14. Is Sue at home?   15. I like apples

16. this is wonderful!   17. here is the book.

SKILLS

Writing a Message   (pages 46–47)

Use the message parts below to write a message.

From Dan   July 6, 1989   To Amy
Meet me at the library on Saturday.
I will be there at 1:00 in the afternoon.

Nouns That Name People, Places, and Things   (pages 54–59)

Write *People*, *Places*, and *Things* at the top of
your paper. Then write each underlined noun under
one of the words.

18. The <u>driver</u> stopped the car.

19. We ate at a very nice <u>restaurant</u>.

20. The cows sleep in the <u>barn</u>.

21. Paul filled a <u>glass</u> with milk.

22. My <u>teacher</u> asked me to help her.

23. The <u>telephone</u> is ringing.

Capitalizing Proper Nouns   (pages 60–63)

Write each special noun correctly.

24. lincoln school   **25.** mr. james rose

26. p. j. brown   **27.** colorado river

ABC Order   (pages 66–67)

Write each group of words in ABC order.

28. hive   drag   mean   star

29. prize   pane   pound   picture

30. wipe   wreck   world   watch

Composition: Letters and Envelopes

CRAFTS FAIR

Patterns
Writing an Invitation
Revising and Proofreading an Invitation
Letter Form
Writing an Envelope
Projects

Grammar, Mechanics, and Usage: Verbs

ACTIVITIES

Action Verbs
Present, Past, and Future Tense
Adding -s to Action Verbs
Words That Sound Alike
Language Play: Baseball Terms
Language and Logic: *Some* Sentences

Practical Language Skills: Vocabulary

ANIMALS

Synonyms and Antonyms
Words That Look Alike

3

Thinking: Patterns

STUDY

Carla is helping her aunt make a quilt for a craft fair. Here are the first three rows of the quilt.

Row 1
Row 2
Row 3

Will the next row look like row 1 or row 2?

REMEMBER

- A **pattern** shows things in a special order.
- Patterns sometimes use colors, shapes, and letters to make a design.

PRACTICE

Completing Patterns Copy and complete each pattern.

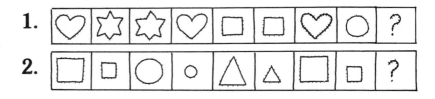

1.
2.

WRITE

Patterns Look at these letter patterns.

AaA BbB CcC   ABc DEf GHi
aBcDeFgHiJk

Then write two letter patterns of your own.

Prewriting: An Invitation

Ted has made a toy plane to show at the craft fair at his school. Ted wants to invite his friend Carlos to the fair. He thinks about the invitation he will write to Carlos.

TOYS! ☆ QUILTS! ☆ RUGS! ☆ BASKETS! ☆ JEWELRY! ☆

WHAT – A CRAFT FAIR
WHERE – GREENLAKE SCHOOL
WHEN – SATURDAY,
OCTOBER 8, 1988
DOORS OPEN AT 9:00
DOORS CLOSE AT 5:00

- ☑ An **invitation** is a letter asking a person to come somewhere.
- ☑ An invitation tells **what, where,** and **when.**

Writing *What, Where, and When* Here are some sentences that Carlos wrote. He plans to use them in his invitation. Copy these sentences. Write *what, where,* or *when* next to each one.

1. Please come to a craft fair.
2. It is being held on April 9, 1988.
3. The fair is at Miller School in room 47.

Sentences Read the article on pages 290–291 of the **DATABANK.** Pretend you are inviting one of these people to your class. Write three sentences. The sentences should tell *what, where,* and *when.*

Writing: An Invitation

Ted thought about his invitation to Carlos. He wanted to make sure he gave all the facts. Ted wrote this invitation.

Date

April 4, 1988

Greeting

Dear Carlos,

Body

Please come to a craft fair at Miller School. The fair will be held on April 9 from 9:00 until 3:00 in room 47. I built a toy plane and a toy boat out of wood. You can see my toys and many other crafts made by children from my school. I hope you can come.

Closing

Your friend,

Signature

Ted

Who wrote this invitation? Who will get the invitation? What is this invitation for?

☑ Begin an invitation with a **date** and a **greeting.**

☑ End an invitation with a **closing** and a **signature.**

Putting an Invitation in Order   Kendra
wants to invite her friend Marie to see a hooked
rug. She begins by listing all of the facts. Read
each fact. Then write an invitation. Put the facts in
the correct order. Use today's date at the top.

PRACTICE

1. Your friend,
   Kendra

2. Please come to a special showing
   of the hooked rug my class made

3. It will be shown from noon
   until 3:00.

4. The rug will be shown on
   Saturday, May 7, at the
   Frost School in room 203.

5. Dear Marie,

An Invitation   Write an invitation to invite
someone to your class. Use today's date. Look
at the sentences you wrote on page 79.

WRITE

Revising: An Invitation

The first time Ted wrote his invitation to Carlos, it was not perfect. Here is the invitation that Ted wrote at first.

PROOFREADING MARKS

∧ add

⊙ period

∧ comma

paragraph indent

≡ capital letter

/ lower-case letter

○ spell correctly

∿ take out

April 4, 1988

Dear Carlos,
   Please come to a craft fair. The fair will be held on April 9 from 9:00 until 3:00. at Miller School in room 47 I built a toy plane out of wood. I built and a toy boat out of wood. You can see my toys and many other crafts made by children from my school. I hope you can come.

                              Your Friend,
                              Ted

Ted found some short sentences in his invitation. He put two sentences together when he could. Find the short sentences Ted changed. What words did Ted add so that Carlos will know where to go? What other words did Ted add?

82

✓ Revise each invitation you write. Ask yourself these questions.

- Did I write *what, where,* and *when?*
- Did I add any missing words?
- Are there short sentences that I can combine?

Revising an Invitation Revise the invitation. Copy it correctly. Put sets of short sentences together. Make sure the invitation tells *what, where,* and *when.*

> September 23, 1988
>
> Dear Josh,
>
> My class is making crafts. I am making crafts. The fair will be held on October 1. The fair begins at noon. The fair ends at 5:00. I hope you can come.
>
> Your friend,
> Susan

A Revised Invitation Revise the invitation you wrote on page 81. Can sets of short sentences be put together? Does the invitation tell *what, where,* and *when?* Change anything you need to.

Proofreading: An Invitation

Editing marks:
- ∧ add
- ⊙ period
- ∧ comma
- ⁋ paragraph indent
- ≡ capital letter
- / lower-case letter
- ꝺ spell correctly
- ℮ take out

In the last lesson you saw Ted's first invitation. He noticed that he made some mistakes. He made some changes to correct them. Next, he proofread the invitation. Look again at Ted's first invitation to see the mistakes he found.

April 4, 1988

Dear Carlos,
    Please come to a craft fair. The fair will   *at Miller School* be held on April 9 from 9:00 until 3:00. *in room 47* I built a toy out of wood. I built a toy boat out of wood. *plane* *and* You can see my toy and many other crafts made *toys* by children from my school. I hope you can come. *hope*
    Your Friend,
    Ted

Notice the editing marks Ted used. The mark ∧ is used to show where a comma is needed. Find the commas that Ted added. What other mistakes did he correct?

84

Proofread each invitation you write. Ask yourself these questions.

- Did I put a comma after the greeting and closing?
- Did I put a comma between the day and the year?
- Did I use capital letters and small letters correctly?
- Did I spell all the words correctly?

Proofread an Invitation   Copy this invitation. Use editing marks to show your corrections.

October 4 1988

Dear Mr. Lewin

Our class is having a craft show on October 23. we would like you to be a judge. The Show will be held from 10:00 until 6:00. It will be in the gym. I hope you can come

Sincerely
Yoko Shira

A Final Copy   Read the invitation you revised in the last lesson. Did you use commas correctly? Correct the letter if you need to.

Make a final copy of your invitation and share it with a friend. Ask your friend if the invitation tells *what*, *where*, and *when*.

Writing: An Envelope

Ted made a neat final copy of his invitation. Then he wrote an envelope to mail it in. He found Carlos's address in the family telephone book. This is Ted's finished envelope.

Ted Clark
225 Elm Street
Carmel, New York 10512

Carlos Mesa
1993 State Street
White Plains, New York 10603

Where on the envelope did Ted write Carlos's address? Where on the envelope did Ted write his own address?

- ☑ Place your own address at the top, left corner of an envelope.
- ☑ Place the address of the person you are writing to in the center of the envelope.
- ☑ Use capital letters to begin the names of places.
- ☑ Use a comma between the city and state.

Revising an Envelope

Copy the envelope that Yoko Shira wrote. Add any missing information.

> 14 Park Lane
> Muir Beach, California 94965
>
> Mr. Paul Lewin
> 414 Brook Street
> San Francisco, 94114

Proofreading an Envelope

Proofread this envelope. Look for mistakes to correct. Write the envelope correctly.

> jane roberts
> 21 yardley Road
> dearborn michigan 48106
>
> Ms. Rhoda Swope
> 48 johnson avenue
> lansing michigan 48924

An Envelope

Write an envelope for your invitation. Use your own address as the return address. Then use another address you know. Revise and proofread the envelope carefully.

Prewrite   Choose a topic for your composition project. You may use one of the topics below or choose one of your own.

Write   Think about what you want to say. Then write your invitation. Be sure your invitation has a date, a greeting, a closing, and a signature.

Revise   Read your invitation and try to make it better. Combine sentences if you can. Check to be sure your invitation tells what, where, and when.

Proofread   Proofread your invitation for mistakes in grammar and spelling. Be sure you use commas, periods, and capital letters correctly. Make a final copy.

Share   Share your writing with others.

Social Studies
Read the facts about airports on pages 302–303 of the **DATABANK.** Pretend you want to invite an airport worker to your class. Write an invitation. Tell the person what information your class wants to learn.

Communications

Write an invitation to the people in your town. Your invitation will be read over the radio. Ask them to come to the opening of a new park. Use the greeting *Dear Radio Listener,* to begin the invitation. End the invitation with the closing *Your friend,* and your name.

Crafts/Hobbies

Pretend that you made a beautiful rug. Write an invitation to a class of children. Ask them to come to see your rug at the fair. Tell what your rug looks like.

Health/Physical Education

Invite a dentist or doctor to your school. Tell what your class would like to learn about good health practices.

Literature

Think of an interesting character from one of your favorite stories. Pretend this character has asked you to a birthday party. Write a letter telling the character that you will be there.

Music/Art

Pretend that you own an art museum. Write an invitation to all museum members. Ask them to come to see a show of new paintings.

Action Verbs

Every sentence has a **verb.** Some verbs show action. An **action verb** tells what someone or something does.

Read the sentences. Notice the words in color.

1. The pitcher throws the ball.
2. Jodie hits the ball.

What does the pitcher do? What does Jodie do? The words *throws* and *hits* are action verbs. They tell what someone does. Read these sentences. Look for the action verbs.

3. The ball flies to the outfield.
4. Jodie runs to the base.

What does the ball do? What does Jodie do? The answers to these questions are action verbs.

Now read these sentences. As you read, ask yourself these questions. What does the coach do? What does Eddie do?

5. The coach talks to the team.
6. Eddie bats next.

☑ Every sentence has a **verb.**
☑ An **action verb** tells what someone or something does.

90

Finding Action Verbs Copy these sentences.
Draw two lines under each action verb.

1. The team plays after school.
2. The players walk onto the field.
3. The coach smiles.
4. The clouds drift away.
5. The crowd waits for the game.
6. Alice pitches the ball.
7. The umpire calls a strike.
8. Alice throws again.
9. Carlos swings and misses.
10. Then Carlos hits the ball and runs to first base.

Writing Action Verbs Copy and complete each sentence. Use each verb in the box only once.

walks	waits	sits	wears	stamp

11. The pitcher ___ to the mound.
12. The coach ___ on the bench.
13. The fans ___ their feet.
14. The umpire ___ a mask.
15. The batter ___ at the plate.

A Message Imagine that you are a coach for a
baseball team. Write a message for your team.
Tell when practice starts. Then tell who pitches
and who catches for the game.

Present Tense

Action verbs can tell when an action takes place. An action verb can name an action that is taking place now. This is called the **present tense of the verb.**

Read these sentences. Look at the words in color.

1. Today the children play soccer.

2. Now one child takes the ball.

What do the children do today? What does one child do now? *Play* and *takes* name actions that are happening now. These action verbs are in the present tense.

Now read these sentences. As you read, look for the action verbs.

3. The players run up the field.

4. Rico kicks the ball.

What do the players do? What does Rico do? The answers to these questions are action verbs. Notice that the actions are happening now. The verbs are in the present tense.

The **present tense** of an action verb names an action that is happening now.

Finding Present-Tense Action Verbs

Read these sentences. Copy the action verb.

1. Two teams go onto the field.
2. The red team kicks the ball.
3. Lee passes to Rico.
4. Rico scores a goal.
5. The fans cheer.
6. The blue team throws in the ball.
7. Two players race after the ball.
8. Who traps the ball?
9. The ball hits someone.
10. The first period ends quickly.

Writing Present-Tense Action Verbs

Copy and complete each sentence. Use each present-tense verb from the box only once.

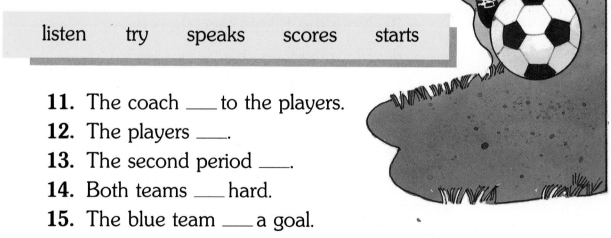

| listen | try | speaks | scores | starts |

11. The coach ____ to the players.
12. The players ____.
13. The second period ____.
14. Both teams ____ hard.
15. The blue team ____ a goal.

A Poem Write a poem about a game you play.
Use an action verb in each sentence. Use present-tense verbs to show actions that happen now.
Your poem does not have to rhyme.

Past Tense

An action verb can name an action that happened in the past. This is called the **past tense of the verb.** Read these sentences. Notice the words in color.

1. Now we climb a mountain.

2. Ella climbed a mountain last week.

Climb names an action that happens now. *Climbed* names an action that happened in the past. What letters were added to the verb *climb* to make *climbed*? To make the past-tense form of many verbs, you add *-ed.*

Read these sentences.

3. Now the hikers lace their boots.

4. Ella laced her boots before.

What verb names an action that happens now? What verb names an action that happened before? What letter was added to the verb *lace* to make *laced*? If a verb ends in *e,* you add only *-d* to form the past tense.

✓ The **past tense** of an action verb shows an action that happened in the past.

✓ Add *-ed* to form the past tense of many verbs.

✓ Add -*d* to verbs that end in *e* to form the past tense.

Finding Past-Tense Action Verbs Read these sentences. Copy each verb that tells about something that happened in the past.

1. The children walked to the park.
2. Mr. Hill meets them at nine.
3. Everyone wears the right clothing.
4. The children hiked all morning.
5. The path turned to the right.
6. A stream crossed the path.
7. Water rushed over the rocks.
8. Ella climbed on the rocks.
9. The water crashed and splashed.
10. The stream twisted and curved.

Using Past-Tense Action Verbs Copy the paragraph. Change each underlined verb to the past tense. Add -*ed* or -*d* to the verb.

The children <u>like</u> their camp. They <u>wait</u> for the animals. Raccoons <u>want</u> food. The animals <u>look</u>. The children <u>watch</u> and <u>listen</u>.

Sentences Read about John Muir on page 306 of the **DATABANK.** Write three sentences about John Muir. Use an action verb in the past tense in each sentence.

Future Tense

STUDY

Action verbs can tell about something that will happen. This is called the **future tense of the verb.** Use *shall* or *will* to make the future tense.

Read these sentences.

1. The children will swim in the lake.

2. I shall row after lunch.

In these sentences, *will swim* and *shall row* are action verbs. Notice that *will* and *shall* have been used with each verb to form the future tense.

Now read the sentences below. Ask yourself these questions. What happens to us tomorrow? What will happen to the girls next week?

3. Tomorrow we shall sail the boat.

4. The girls will paddle the canoe next week.

Notice that *shall sail* and *will paddle* name actions that will happen in the future. *Shall* or *will* comes before the verb in the future tense.

REMEMBER

- ✓ The **future tense** names an action that will happen in the future.
- ✓ Use *shall* or *will* before the verb to make the future tense.
- ✓ Use *shall* when the subject is *I* or *we.*

96

Finding Future-Tense Action Verbs
Copy each sentence that has an action verb in the future tense.

1. We shall fish tomorrow.
2. You will need a pole.
3. All the children will come.
4. Who will bring food?
5. Luanne will pack lunch.
6. I like picnic lunches.
7. I packed the lunch last year.
8. You will enjoy the boat ride.
⭐ 9. Who will take us?
⭐ 10. How many fish will you catch?

Using Future-Tense Action Verbs
Write each sentence. Write each underlined verb in the future tense.

11. Fish <u>nibble</u> at sunset.
12. We <u>need</u> bait.
13. The breezes <u>feel</u> cool.
14. The waves <u>splash</u>.
15. The children <u>grow</u> sleepy.

Sentences   Imagine that tomorrow you will go to a lake or a park. Write three sentences telling what you will do there. Use an action verb in the future tense in each sentence.

Adding -*s* to Action Verbs

Some action verbs tell what one person or thing does. Other action verbs tell what more than one person or thing does.

Read these sentences. Notice the action verbs in color.

1. One horse stands quietly.
2. Two horses stand together.

The action verb *stands* tells what one horse does. The action verb *stand* tells what more than one horse does. A present-tense action verb that tells about one person or thing ends in -*s*.

Read the sentences below. As you read, ask yourself these questions. Which verb tells what one person does? Which verb tells what two people do? Which verb ends in -*s*?

3. Jim rides well.

4. Jim and Sid ride together.

✓ Add -*s* to a present-tense action verb to tell about one person or thing.

98

Finding Verbs   Read these sentences. Copy each sentence that tells about one person or thing. Underline the verb.

1. These horses run fast.
2. This horse takes me far.
3. Some saddles hang in the barn.
4. My saddle hangs in the barn.
5. The blacksmith comes in the spring.
6. Most blacksmiths love horses.
7. Vets care for horses.
8. One vet lives nearby.
9. He visits once a month.
10. The horses receive good care.

Writing Verbs   Copy and complete each sentence. Use each action verb from the box only once.

stand	ride	eats	sleeps	eat

11. Horses ___ grass and grain.
12. Nellie ___ every day.
13. I ___ Nellie before breakfast.
14. The horse ___ in the barn.
15. The haystacks ___ in the field.

A Conversation   Imagine that you have two talking horses. Write a conversation in which you talk about something you all like to do.

Words That Are Easily Confused

Some words sound alike. But they may have different spellings and different meanings.

Read these sentences.

1. Do the children know the way?

2. No, they don't.

What two words sound alike? *Know* and *no* sound alike. The two words are spelled differently. Which word means "understand"? Which word means "the opposite of yes"? *Know* means "understand." *No* means "the opposite of yes."

Read the sentences below. Find the two words that sound alike.

3. My bicycle is new.

4. I knew that.

New and *knew* sound alike. You can tell which word to use in each sentence if you understand what each word means. *New* means "not old." *Knew* means "understood."

- Some words that sound alike have different spellings and different meanings.
- You can tell which word to use if you understand what each word means.

Finding the Meaning of Sound-Alike Words

Copy these sentences. Write the word or words that mean the same as the underlined word.

1. You will find your bike <u>by</u> the tree.
   a. get with money   b. beside

2. There were <u>eight</u> bikes.
   a. had a meal   b. the number after seven

3. I did not <u>hear</u> the car.
   a. listen   b. in this place

4. Make a <u>right</u> turn.
   a. make letters or words   b. the opposite of left

5. Our team <u>won</u> the race.
   a. the number before two   b. finished first

Writing Sound-Alike Words   Copy each

sentence. Write the correct word.

6. We will meet ___ .   hear   here
7. Your team is number ___ .   one   won
8. We ___ after the race.   eight   ate
9. Is that water ___ you?   for   four
10. Do you ___ everyone?   know   no

A Riddle   Use the words *won* and *one* to write a riddle.

How Can You Steal Home?

STUDY

Sometimes the terms used in sports can bring funny pictures to your mind. If someone told you to steal home in a baseball game, what would you do? Would you try to run to home base between pitches? Would you try to pick up home base and run away with it? What do you think the baseball term *stealing home* really means?

PRACTICE

Choosing the Right Term   The pictures below are funny ways to show the baseball terms in the box. Choose a term to go under each picture. Then write the terms on a piece of paper.

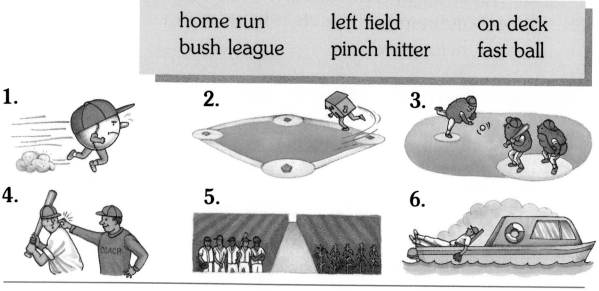

home run	left field	on deck
bush league	pinch hitter	fast ball

1.

2.

3.

4.

5.

6.

WRITE

Writing a Letter   Write a funny letter to a friend. Tell how someone on a baseball team became confused by a baseball term.

Language and Logic

Sentences With *All*

Look at the picture. Then read sentence 1.

1. All of the cats have tails.

All means "every one." You see that every cat in the picture has a tail. So sentence 1 is true. Now read sentence 2.

2. All of the cats are black.

You see that not every cat is black. Some of the cats are not black. So sentence 2 is false.

Classifying Sentences With *All*   Read these

sentences. Write *true* if the sentence is true. Write *false* if the sentence is false.

1. All of the cats have four legs.

2. All of the cats have spots.

3. All of the cats have fur.

★ **4.** All cats have fur.

★ **5.** All dogs are fish.

Synonyms and Antonyms

STUDY

Read these two sentences. The words in color mean almost the same thing.

1. That is a small cat.
2. That is a little cat.

Words that mean almost the same thing are called **synonyms.** *Small* and *little* are synonyms. You can use synonyms to make your writing more interesting.

Now read these sentences. The words in color mean opposite things.

3. That dog is a large animal.
4. This mouse is a small animal.

Words that have opposite meanings are called **antonyms.** *Large* and *small* are antonyms. You can use antonyms to show how two things are different.

REMEMBER

- **Synonyms** are words that mean almost the same thing. Use synonyms to make your writing more interesting.

- **Antonyms** are words that have opposite meanings. Use antonyms to tell how two things are different.

104

Finding Synonyms and Antonyms

Read each pair of words. Write *synonym* if the words have almost the same meaning. Write *antonym* if the words have opposite meanings.

1. angry   mad
2. laugh   cry
3. speak   talk
4. sleepy   tired
5. high   low

Using Synonyms and Antonyms

Look at the words in the box. Find a synonym or an antonym for each underlined word. Write the sentence using the new word.

wonderful	enjoyed	speak
foolish		tame

6. I want to <u>tell</u> about our pet show.
7. We all had a <u>terrible</u> time.
8. All of the animals in the show were <u>wild</u>.
9. We all <u>liked</u> the dog parade.
10. The cats looked <u>ridiculous</u> in the pink bows.

A Description

Read pages 300–301 in the **DATABANK** to learn about some unusual pets. Choose two pets you would like. Write three sentences about each pet. Use synonyms or antonyms where you can.

Frequently Confused Words

Read these sentences. Look at the words in color. They are spelled the same.

1. The rooster has a loud crow.
2. A big, black crow flew by.

Some words are spelled the same but mean different things. Do the words in color mean the same thing? Which word means the sound a rooster makes? Which word means a large black bird? How can you tell?

Some words are spelled the same but sound different and mean different things. *Wind* can rhyme with *mind* or with *pinned.* Which sound does *wind* have in each sentence below? What does *wind* mean in each sentence?

3. The wind made the kite fly high.
4. Did you wind the kite string?

✓ Some words are spelled the same but mean different things.

✓ Some words are spelled the same but sound different and mean different things.

106

Matching Pictures and Meanings

Choose the meaning that matches each picture. Write the meaning.

1.
   a. hit
   b. small animal

2.
   a. piece of wood
   b. attach

3.
   a. near
   b. shut

4.
   a. knot with loops
   b. bend

Choosing the Meaning

Read each sentence. Choose the correct meaning for the underlined word. Write the meaning.

5. The <u>duck</u> swims in the pond.
   a. water bird   b. to lower your head

6. The chicken coop is one <u>story</u> high.
   a. tale   b. floor

7. One goose will <u>fly</u> ahead of the others.
   a. insect   b. travel through air

8. That goose will <u>lead</u> the other geese.
   a. show the way for   b. metal

Sentences

Write two sentences. Use these different meanings of the word *light*.
- not heavy
- lamp

Composition   Write an invitation to a friend. Ask your friend to come to a performance that will be given by your school band.

Grammar, Mechanics, and Usage   Choose the correct way to write each example.

1. ⓐ Dear Mr. Parks   ⓑ Dear Mr. Parks,
2. ⓐ Your friend,   ⓑ Your friend
3. ⓐ Austin Texas 78700,   ⓑ Austin, Texas 78700

Choose the action verb in each sentence.

4. I <u>walk</u> to <u>school</u>.
   ⓐ ⓑ ⓒ ⓓ

5. The <u>red</u> <u>rooster</u> <u>crows</u>.
   ⓐ ⓑ ⓒ ⓓ

6. The <u>two</u> <u>girls</u> <u>swim</u>.
   ⓐ ⓑ ⓒ ⓓ

7. <u>Ken</u> <u>plays</u> <u>the</u> <u>piano</u>.
   ⓐ ⓑ ⓒ ⓓ

Choose the tense of the underlined verb in each sentence.

8. I <u>will draw</u> a picture.
   ⓐ past ⓑ present
   ⓒ future

9. The dog <u>barked</u> at Ben.
   ⓐ past ⓑ present
   ⓒ future

10. Ron <u>sees</u> a plane.
    ⓐ past ⓑ present
    ⓒ future

11. Rashid <u>called</u> my name.
    ⓐ past ⓑ present
    ⓒ future

Choose the correct verb to complete each sentence.

12. We ___ the bags.
    ⓐ hold   ⓑ holds

13. Ned ___ the wagon.
    ⓐ pull   ⓑ pulls

14. I ___ the paper.
    ⓐ cut   ⓑ cuts

15. My pets ___ here.
    ⓐ sleep   ⓑ sleeps

Choose the correct word to complete each sentence.

16. The sky is ___.
    ⓐ blew   ⓑ blue

17. Is the ___ done?
    ⓐ meat   ⓑ meet

18. I will ___ a letter.
    ⓐ write   ⓑ right

19. ___ boys play ball.
    ⓐ Four   ⓑ For

Practical Language Skills Choose the words that mean almost the same thing.

20. ⓐ frown, smile   ⓑ cold, chilly   ⓒ quiet, loud

21. ⓐ light, dark   ⓑ near, far   ⓒ forest, woods

Choose the words that have opposite meanings.

22. ⓐ sad, cheerful   ⓑ keep, save   ⓒ jump, hop

23. ⓐ huge, big   ⓑ happy, glad   ⓒ close, open

Choose the meaning for the underlined word in each sentence.

24. The dog has a loud <u>bark</u>.
    ⓐ the covering on a tree   ⓑ a short, sharp sound

25. Jenny tied a <u>bow</u> on the package.
    ⓐ a knot that has loops   ⓑ bend the head or body

Composition: Personal Narrative

HOLIDAYS AND CELEBRATIONS

Sequencing
Writing a Paragraph That Tells a Story
Revising and Proofreading a Paragraph
  That Tells a Story
Capitalization of Holidays
Projects

Grammar, Mechanics, and Usage: Nouns

SHOPPING

Singular and Plural Nouns
Forming Plurals
Rules for Capitalization
Sentence Combining: Subjects
Language Play: Making New Words

Practical Language Skills: Speaking and Listening

RADIO AND TV

Purposeful Listening
Oral Summaries
Giving Directions

4

Thinking: Sequencing

Valentine's Day is coming soon. Linda wants to send a valentine to a friend. First, Linda makes a valentine. Next, she writes a message on the valentine. What does Linda do last?

☑ Things we do and stories we read have a **beginning,** a **middle,** and an **end.**

☑ Telling about things in **time order** can make them easier to understand.

Writing Sentences in Order   Read the sentences. Write them in the correct time order.

1. Next, Mark's Dad carves the pumpkin.
2. First, Mark buys a pumpkin.
3. Last of all, Mark puts the pumpkin in the window.

A Comic Strip   Draw a comic strip with three pictures. Show the beginning, middle, and end of a story. Write sentences above the heads of the characters in your comic strip.

Prewriting: A Paragraph That Tells a Story

Adam and his family went to see a parade on Columbus Day. Now Adam wants to write about the day. Adam thinks about what he did at the beginning, middle, and end of the day. Then he writes a paragraph.

- A **paragraph** is a group of sentences that tells about one thing.
- A paragraph that tells a story often tells about things in time order.

Using Time Order   The sentences below are from Adam's paragraph. Copy them. Decide where each sentence is in the paragraph. Write *beginning, middle,* or *end* next to each sentence.

1. First, I went to the city with my parents.
2. Last of all, I ate dinner at a restaurant.
3. Next, I watched a big parade.

Sentences   Read the poems about holidays on pages 284–285 of the **DATABANK.** Think about a holiday that you enjoy. Write three sentences about what you usually do on the holiday. The sentences should tell about things in time order.

Writing: A Paragraph That Tells a Story

Peg wants to remember all the fun she had on the Fourth of July. Peg writes this paragraph so she can remember what she did on this holiday.

> The Fourth of July was a lot of fun! First, my parents and I went swimming at a lake near our home. Next, we ate a picnic dinner as the sun set. Last of all, we watched a beautiful fireworks show at the lake. We also planned another picnic dinner for Labor Day.

What is this paragraph about?

- ☑ **Indent** the first word in a paragraph. Move it a few spaces to the right.
- ☑ The **main idea** sentence tells what the paragraph is about. Begin a paragraph with a main idea sentence.
- ☑ Use **signal words** such as *first*, *next*, and *last*. These words tell about the order in which things happen.

Telling the Main Idea and Using Signal Words   Sam wrote these sentences telling what his family did on Thanksgiving.

> Last of all, we gathered around the piano to sing songs together.
>
> First, we all helped fix the meal.
>
> Next, we sat down to eat a big turkey dinner.

    Pretend you are Sam. Write a paragraph using his sentences. Begin the paragraph with a sentence that tells the main idea. Then put Sam's sentences in order using his signal words. Remember to indent the first word in the paragraph.

Writing a Paragraph That Tells a Story
Write a paragraph using Adam's sentences from page 113. Be sure to add a sentence that tells the main idea. Do not forget to indent the first word in the paragraph.

A Paragraph   Read the sentences you wrote on page 113. Use them to write a paragraph about a holiday you enjoy. Begin your paragraph with a sentence that tells the main idea.

Revising: A Paragraph That Tells a Story

Peg's paragraph was not perfect the first time she wrote it. Here is the paragraph Peg wrote at first. Notice the changes in red.

add ∧

period ⊙

comma ∧,

paragraph indent ¶

capital letter ≡

lower-case letter /

spell correctly ◯

take out ℓ

> The fourth of july was a lot of fun! First∧ My parents, and I went swimming at a lake near our home. ~~I went swimming at a lake near our home.~~ Next∧ We ate a picnic dinner as the sun set. Last of all∧ We watched a beautiful fireworks show at the lake. We also planned another ◯picnic◯ dinner for labor day.

Peg found that she forgot to use signal words. Then she saw that the second and third sentences had the same predicate. She joined these sentences together.

What signal words did Peg add? What sentences did Peg join together?

◢ Revise your paragraph. Ask yourself these questions.
- Did I use signal words where they are needed?
- Are there sentences that I can combine?

116

Combining Sentences Read each pair of sentences. Combine each pair of short sentences into a longer sentence.

1. My sister wanted to go on a picnic.
   I wanted to go on a picnic.

2. Dad made peanut butter sandwiches.
   Jenny made peanut butter sandwiches.

3. Mom packed the picnic basket.
   I packed the picnic basket.

4. The sandwiches were delicious.
   The lemonade and fruit were delicious.

Revising a Paragraph That Tells a Story

Copy this paragraph. Look for short sentences that can be combined. Add signal words to help make the order clear.

I planned my own birthday party this year. I wrote invitations to all my friends. My sister made muffins and popcorn. I made muffins and popcorn. Mom helped me put up streamers.

A Revised Paragraph Revise the paragraph that you wrote for the **Write** activity on page 115. Did you write about things in order? Did you use signal words? Can you join any of the sentences together? Change anything you need to.

Proofreading: A Paragraph That Tells a Story

STUDY

Editing marks:
- ∧ add
- ⊙ period
- ∧, comma
- ⌗ paragraph indent
- ≡ capital letter
- / lower-case letter
- ∽ spell correctly
- ℓ take out

On page 116 you looked at some of the changes Peg made in her paragraph. Peg also proofread her paragraph. Look again at Peg's first paragraph to see what mistakes she found. Notice the changes in red.

First∧ The fourth of july was a lot of fun! ∧My parents∧ and I went swimming at a lake near our home. I went swimming at a lake near our home. Next∧ We ate a picnic dinner as the sun set. Last of all∧ We watched a beautiful *beautiful* fireworks show at the lake. We also planned another *picnic* picnick dinner for labor day.

Peg knows that each important word in a holiday should begin with a capital letter. Notice the editing marks that she used. The editing mark ≡ shows where a capital letter is needed. The editing mark / shows where a small letter is needed.

What letters did Peg change from small to capital? What letters did Peg change from capital to small?

Peg also corrected some spelling mistakes. Can you find the two words that Peg corrected?

118

Proofread your work. Ask yourself these questions.

- Did I use capital letters and small letters correctly?
- Did I spell all the words correctly?

Correcting a Paragraph Copy Peg's paragraph. Make all the changes that Peg marked.

Proofreading a Paragraph That Describes
Copy this paragraph and correct it. Use editing marks to show your corrections.

   Last year I sent some silly Holiday cards to my friend Jack. First I sent him a funny valentine's day card. Next I sent him a card with a riddle on it for april fool's day. Last of all, I made a card that looked like a pumkin. i sent it to Jack for halloween.

A Final Copy Proofread the paragraph that you revised in the **Write** activity on page 117. Did you capitalize the first letter of each important word in the holiday? Correct the paragraph if you need to. Use editing marks to show your corrections. Make a final copy of your paragraph.

Read your paragraph to a friend. Ask your friend if the paragraph tells about things in the correct time order.

Composition Projects

Prewrite   Choose one of the topics below for your composition project. You may also choose a topic of your own. Begin by making a list or talking to other people about your topic.

Write   Begin with a sentence that tells what your paragraph is about. Be sure your paragraph tells about things in correct time order.

Revise   Read your paragraph again and try to make it better. Check to be sure you have used signal words such as *first, next,* and *last* to show time order. Combine short sentences if you can.

Proofread   Read your paragraph again. Proofread it to make sure you have used capital letters and small letters correctly. Correct any spelling or grammar mistakes. Make a final copy of your paragraph.

Share   Share your paragraph with others.

Science
Read the poems about weather on pages 286–287 of the **DATABANK**. Think about a time when you were caught in a thunderstorm, a rainstorm, or a snowstorm. Write a paragraph telling what you did during the storm.

Communications

Pretend that your school newspaper has asked you to write about a vacation. Write a paragraph telling about the trip.

Health/Physical Education

Think of a time when you played on a winning team. Write a paragraph telling what and how your team won.

Literature

A diary is a written record of things that happen to a person every day. Write a paragraph that could be used in a diary. Tell about three things that your class did in school today. Write them in the correct time order.

Mathematics

Pretend that you are watching a construction project. Write a paragraph that tells what happens as the building goes up.

Music/Art

Pretend you are a piece of music. Write a paragraph explaining how you should sound. Explain how your beginning, middle, and end should be played. Use the signal words *beginning, middle,* and *end* in your paragraph.

Singular and Plural Nouns

You know that nouns name people, places, and things. Read these sentences. Notice the nouns in color.

1. The girl is busy.
2. The girls are busy.

What noun names one person? What noun names more than one person? The noun *girl* names one. It is a **singular noun**. The noun *girls* names more than one. It is a **plural noun**.

Now read these sentences.

3. The ball fell.
4. The balls fell.

Which noun is singular? Which noun is plural? What letter was added to *ball* to form *balls*?

- ☑ A **singular noun** names one person, place, or thing.
- ☑ A **plural noun** names more than one person, place, or thing.
- ☑ Plural nouns often end in s.

122

Labeling Nouns Read these sentences. Copy each noun. Write *singular* if the noun names one. Write *plural* if the noun names more than one.

1. All of the stores are crowded.
2. Come with me to the store.
3. Look at the games.
4. I like the stickers.
⭐ 5. Choose a car or a truck.

Choosing Nouns Copy these sentences. Choose the correct noun in ( ).

6. Cara bought a (gift, gifts).
7. She looked at two (boat, boats).
8. She chose a red (boat, boats).
9. Lee wanted a (truck, trucks).
10. He asked a (clerk, clerks) for help.
11. Lee bought two green (truck, trucks).
12. Lee showed Gary three (game, games).
13. Amy had one (dollar, dollars).
⭐ 14. She saw several (thing, things) she liked.
⭐ 15. Did Amy buy two (ball, balls) or a (bat, bats)?

A Poster Make a poster showing things you might see in a toy store. At the bottom write four sentences about these things. Use two singular nouns and two plural nouns in your sentences.

Forming Plurals

Most plural nouns end in s. However, some nouns are different. Read these sentences. Notice the nouns in color.

1. The bus came.
2. The buses came.

Which noun is singular? Which noun is plural? *Bus* is singular. *Buses* is plural. What letters were added to *bus* to form *buses*?

Some nouns end in s. Other nouns end in *x*, *ss*, *ch*, or *sh*. To form their plurals, add *-es*.

Now read these sentences. Notice the nouns in color.

3. A family waited.
4. Two families waited.

The singular noun is *family*. The plural noun is *families*. What is the last letter of *family*? What spelling change is made to form *families*?

Some nouns end in *y*. Make a spelling change to form the plural. Change the *y* to *i* and add *-es*.

☑ Add *-es* to form the plural of nouns that end in *s*, *x*, *ss*, *ch*, or *sh*.

☑ Change the *y* to *i* and add *-es* to form the plural of most nouns that end in *y*.

124

Writing Plural Nouns   Write the plural form for each noun.

PRACTICE

1. berry
2. bush
3. lunch
4. fox
5. brush
6. stitch
7. wish
8. match
9. diary
10. buzz

Using Plural Nouns   Write these sentences. Write the plural form for each underlined noun.

11. People sat on the <u>bench</u>.
12. They waited near the <u>bush</u>.
13. The <u>watch</u> ticked loudly.
14. The <u>glass</u> had a pretty design.
15. The <u>dish</u> looked colorful.
16. We put cards in the <u>mailbox</u>.
17. We looked at the <u>dress</u>.
18. The bag held the tiny <u>pony</u>.
19. The <u>family</u> spoke to the <u>baby</u>.
20. The <u>box</u> seemed safe on the <u>bus</u>.

An Advertisement

Write an advertisement telling about things you might see in a gift shop. Use a plural noun from the lesson in each sentence.

WRITE

Irregular Plurals

Many plural nouns end in *s* or *es*. However, the plural for some nouns is formed in a different way.

Read these sentences. Notice the nouns in color.

1. The child looked.

2. The children looked.

Which noun names one person? Which noun names more than one person?

The noun *child* is singular. The noun *children* is plural. The plural is formed by changing the spelling. Here are some other nouns. You must make a spelling change to form the plural.

man—men	tooth—teeth	ox—oxen
woman—women	foot—feet	mouse—mice

Now read the sentences below. Look for the nouns. As you read, ask yourself these questions. Which noun is singular? Which noun is plural?

3. We saw one black goose.

4. Three white geese ran away.

◢ You must make a spelling change to form the plural of some nouns.

126

Writing Plural Nouns Write the plural form
of each noun.

1. child
2. goose
3. man
4. foot
5. woman
6. tooth
7. mouse
8. ox

Writing Plural Nouns Copy the paragraph.
Write a word from the box on each line. Use each
word only once.

feet	men	children
geese	mice	women

The ___ were excited. The ___ and ___
cheered. Girls and boys stamped their ___. ___
ran away. The ___ were having a race.

A Story Imagine that a mouse, a goose, or an
ox told you a story. Write the story that the
animal told you. Use three plural nouns from this
lesson in your story.

Capitalization of Nouns

Some nouns begin with capital letters. Read these sentences.

1. Mrs. Irma T. Hall owns a store.

2. The store is on Main Street.

Who owns a store? What title is used in the name? What is the initial? *Mrs. Irma T. Hall* owns the store. Her title is *Mrs.* Her initial is *T.* The name and the title begin with a capital letter. The initial is written with a capital letter.

Where is the store? The store is on Main Street. *Main Street* names a special place. Each word in the name begins with a capital letter.

Now read these sentences. Look for the special nouns.

3. The store opened in May.

4. We went there on Saturday.

5. It was closed on Memorial Day.

What noun names a month? What noun names a day? What noun names a holiday?

- ☑ Write names, titles, and initials with capital letters.
- ☑ Write special place names with capital letters.
- ☑ Begin days of the week, months of the year, and holidays with capital letters.

Capitalizing Nouns Write each noun correctly.

1. november
2. maria martinez
3. tuesday
4. r. j. smith
5. mr. eng
6. broad avenue
7. dr. ella wentworth
8. riverside square
9. united states
10. flag day

Capitalizing Nouns Write the paragraph. Use capital letters where they are needed.

Every monday we shop on main street. Our first stop is best foods. This week we are shopping for thanksgiving. We are having a big dinner with aunt sally and uncle bob. They will be staying with us until the middle of december.

A Map Draw a map. Show how to get to a store from your house. Write the directions. Use the names of four special places.

Sentence Combining: Subjects

Every sentence has a naming part, or **subject**.
Every sentence has a telling part, or **predicate**.
Sometimes two sentences have the same predicate.
Then you can join the subjects.

Read these sentences.

1. Rosa saw the dog.

2. Eddie saw the dog.

What is the subject of each sentence? What is the predicate of each sentence?

Subject	Predicate
Rosa	
	saw the dog
Eddie	

You can join the subjects to form a new sentence. The word *and* joins the two subjects.

3. Rosa and Eddie saw the dog.

Read the sentence below. What is the predicate? What two subjects have been joined?

4. Boys and girls visited the pet store.

▰ If two sentences have the same predicate, the subjects can be joined.

▰ Use *and* to join two subjects.

Finding Sentences With Two Subjects

Read these sentences. Copy only the sentences that have two subjects joined together. Ring the two subjects.

1. Flora and Juan go to the pet store.
2. Jesse sees a bird in a cage.
3. A puppy and a kitten are friendly.
4. The rabbit is soft and cute.
⭐ 5. Boys and girls talk to the parrot.

Combining Sentences

Read each pair of sentences. Make a new sentence by joining the two subjects together.

6. Puppies play happily.
   Kittens play happily.
7. Turtles live here.
   Goldfish live here.
8. Chicks need food.
   Birds need food.
9. Seeds are good for birds.
   Berries are good for birds.
⭐ 10. Mother ducks quack.
   Their babies quack.

Sentences

Imagine that you have two pets. Write two sentences about your pets. In each sentence, join two subjects together. Read pages 300–301 of the **DATABANK**. It gives facts about pets.

Language Play

Missing Letters

STUDY

*Please Leave
Your Grocery
art Here*

When Dan first looks at the sign in the grocery store, he is confused. He does not know what *Grocery art* is. Then Luis moves away from the sign. What do you think the sign really says? What letter is Dan unable to read?

You can often make another word by taking out one letter from the word.

PRACTICE

Making New Words   Copy each word below. Take out one letter from each word to make a new word. You may take out a letter from the beginning, middle, or end of the word. Then write each new word next to the old word.

1. shop
2. cost
3. price
4. meat
5. cash
6. can
7. box
8. store
9. tax
10. pear
11. mart
12. stack
★13. orange
★14. aisle
★15. wrapper

WRITE

Writing a Paragraph   Pretend you have just made a trip to the grocery store. Write a paragraph about your trip. Use at least five of the words above.

Language and Logic

Sentences With *None*

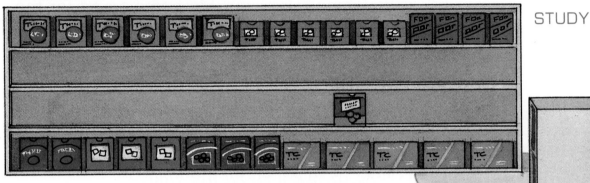

Look at the picture. Then read sentence 1.

    1. None of the boxes are red.

None means "not a single one." You see that there is not a single red box. So sentence 1 is true.
    Now read sentence 2.

    2. None of the boxes are green.

You see some green boxes. So sentence 2 is false.

Classifying Sentences With *None* Read

these sentences. Write *true* if the sentence is true. Write *false* if the sentence is false.

    1. None of the boxes are yellow.

    2. None of the boxes are blue.

    3. None of the boxes are on the top shelf.

    4. None of the boxes are on the second shelf.

    5. None of the boxes are red.

    6. None of the shelves are empty.

Purposeful Listening

Ted is watching television. He hears an ad for the Greenville Zoo. Ted wants to learn more about the zoo. He listens to the ad carefully. This is what Ted hears.

"Why not have some fun today?
Visit Greenville Zoo.
Follow us, we'll show the way.
You'll find a lot to see and do.

The monkeys here will make you laugh.
The bears will make you roar.
Ride a camel, feed a giraffe.
See tigers, seals—and more!"

What is the ad asking Ted to do? This is the **main idea** of the ad. What animals will Ted see at the zoo? To find information like this, listen for **details.** Look at the last word in each line. Which words end the same way? These words **rhyme.**

- ✓ When you listen, try to find the **main idea** of the speaker's words.
- ✓ Pay attention to the **details** that tell you about the main idea.
- ✓ When you listen for **rhyme,** listen to the ending sounds of words.

134

Reading for Main Idea, Detail, and Rhyme

Read this ad. Write answers to the questions.

"Barker's Wheat Bread tastes the best.
You'll find it better than the rest.
It's always fresh and never dry.
It's the best bread you can buy!"

1. What is this ad about?
2. What are two details that are given in the ad?
3. Which words in the ad rhyme?

Listening for Main Idea, Detail, and Rhyme

Listen as your teacher reads an ad to you. As you listen, ask yourself these questions. Then write your answers.

4. What is this ad about?
5. What are three details that are given in the ad?
6. What are four words that rhyme in the ad?

An Ad Write a rhyming ad for the radio. Then choose a partner to listen to your ad. Ask your partner to tell what the ad is about. Ask your partner to name the words that rhyme. Then listen to your partner's ad and answer the same questions.

Oral Summaries

Susan is listening to the radio. Her mother has asked her to listen and give a **summary** of the news. Susan hears this news report.

"A large storm hit the town of Highland last night. The storm began at 7:00 in the evening and ended at 10:00. Many trees were knocked down on Main Street and Turner Street. The homes in Highland had no lights or water for four hours after the storm hit. Mayor Gordon said that it was one of the worst storms ever to hit Highland."

Susan knows that a summary is a short retelling. It gives only the important facts. Susan begins her summary with the main idea of what she heard. What was the main idea of the news report? Then she adds the most important details. Here is Susan's summary.

"A large storm hit the town of Highland last night. Many trees were knocked down. Highland was without lights and water."

136

☑ A **summary** is a short retelling.

☑ Include the main idea and some important details of the information you want to summarize.

Understanding a Summary Copy Susan's summary. Draw one line under the main idea. Draw two lines under each detail.

Writing a Summary Pretend you have just heard this report on the radio. Write a summary of the report. Read it aloud.

"A new park has just opened in the city of Salem. The park is on the corner of Main Street and Elm Street. The park has a large playground with swings, slides, a wooden fort, and a baseball diamond. The park also has a shady picnic area where people can relax and enjoy a picnic lunch."

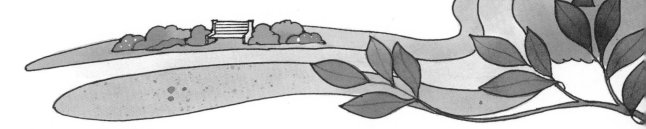

A News Report Write a news report about something that happened in your town. Then choose a partner. Give your partner the report. Ask your partner to read the report and give a summary of it. Then read your partner's report. Give a summary of that report.

Giving Directions

Jenny wants to record her voice on Sam's tape recorder. She does not know how to use the tape recorder. She asks Sam for help. Sam explains how to use the tape recorder. He tries to use words that are clear and easy to understand. He tells Jenny what to do in the order in which she must do it. Here are Sam's **directions** to Jenny.

"First check that the microphone is plugged into the tape recorder. Next press the button marked EJECT. That opens the tape recorder. Then put a tape into the tape recorder. Close the cover. Last of all, press the buttons marked PLAY and RECORD. Talk into the microphone."

What is the first thing Jenny must do? What is the last thing Jenny must do?

- Use clear words that are easy to understand when you give **directions.**
- Tell each step in the correct order.

138

Reading Directions   Read both sets of directions. Copy the set of directions that is written correctly.

1. First, pick up the receiver on the telephone. Then, call the number you want. Listen for a dial tone before you dial the number.

2. First, move the large dial to the words SET ALARM. Next, set the time you want to wake up. Last of all, move the large dial to the words RADIO ALARM.

Ordering Directions   The sentences below tell how to listen to a tape that has been recorded. Write the directions in order.

3. Last of all, press the PLAY button to hear what you have recorded.

4. After you unplug the microphone, press the REWIND button.

5. Then, wait for the tape to rewind.

6. First, unplug the microphone.

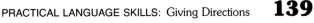

A Set of Directions   Look at the picture of the recorder on page 269 of the **DATABANK.** Write directions telling how to use this recorder. Read them to a friend and ask if the directions are clear and easy to understand.

Composition   Write a short paragraph that tells about an interesting place you have visited.

Grammar, Mechanics, and Usage   Choose *one* or *more than one* to tell how many each underlined noun names.

1. The <u>girls</u> climb trees.
   (a) one
   (b) more than one

2. The <u>boy</u> likes to swim.
   (a) one
   (b) more than one

3. The <u>cars</u> are parked.
   (a) one
   (b) more than one

4. The <u>store</u> is closed.
   (a) one
   (b) more than one

Choose the correct plural form for each underlined noun.

5. The <u>box</u> is full.
   (a) boxs   (b) boxes

6. Please cut the <u>bush</u>.
   (a) bushes   (b) bushies

7. My <u>pony</u> is brown.
   (a) ponys   (b) ponies

8. a <u>lady</u> helped me.
   (a) ladies   (b) ladys

9. Tim's <u>foot</u> hurt.
   (a) foots   (b) feet

10. The <u>child</u> is playing.
    (a) childs   (b) children

11. The <u>mouse</u> is tiny.
    (a) mice   (b) mouses

12. Esther's <u>tooth</u> is lose.
    (a) tooths   (b) teeth

Chooose the correct way to write each noun.

13. (a) ms. Rita Lopez   (b) Ms. rita lopez
    (c) Ms. Rita Lopez   (d) ms. rita lopez

14. (a) Lake street   (b) Lake Street
    (c) lake street   (d) lake Street

15. (a) Fourth of july   (b) fourth of july
     (c) fourth of July   (d) Fourth of July

Choose the sentence from which the example was made.

16. Sam and I played ball.
    (a) Sam played ball.   (b) Sam played ball.
       I watched him.   We played ball.
    (c) He played ball.   (d) Sam played ball.
       I played ball.   I played ball.

17. Mom and Dad cooked dinner.
    (a) Mom cooked dinner.   (b) They cooked dinner.
       Dad cooked dinner.   Mom cooked dinner.
    (c) Mom cooked dinner.   (d) She cooked dinner.
       Dad baked bread.   He cooked dinner.

Practical Language Skills   Choose the best ending
for each sentence.

18. To find rhyming words, listen to the ___.
    (a) beginning of words.   (b) end of words.
    (c) main idea.   (d) small details

19. Begin a summary by telling the ___.
    (a) small details.   (b) day and time.
    (c) main idea.   (d) rhyming words.

20. When you give directions, use ___.
    (a) clear words   (b) rhyming words
    (c) hard words   (d) steps out of order

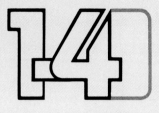

Parts of a Sentence   (pages 5–7, 28–29)

Copy the sentences. Ring the subject of each sentence. Underline the predicate.

1. John ran to the park.
2. Ken is at school.
3. The girls are happy.
4. The women work hard.

Guide Words   (pages 68–69)

Write a word that would be found on the same page as each pair of guide words below.

5. lunch/mean
6. prize/reach
7. bold/cent

Writing an Invitation   (pages 80–81)

Write an invitation. Use the letter parts below.

Your friend,   Dear Tina,

Please come to a party at my house.

Ben   December 2, 1988

The party will begin at 2:00 on December 10, 1988.

Verb Tense   (pages 90–95)

Copy the sentences. Then write *past, present,* or *future* to tell the tense of each underlined verb.

8. I <u>showed</u> Dad my work.
9. Jenny <u>shall visit</u> me tomorrow.
10. I <u>like</u> the monkeys at the zoo.

142

SKILLS

Words That Sound Alike   (pages 98–99)

Choose the word that completes each sentence. Then write the sentence on your paper.

11. The wind (blue, blew) the hat off my head.

12. There are many cars on the (rode, road).

Synonyms and Antonyms   (pages 102–105)

Copy each pair of words. Underline the pairs of words that are synonyms. Ring the pairs of words that are antonyms.

13. old/new

14. frightened/scared

15. crying/laughing

16. dark/light

17. loud/noisy

18. high/tall

Writing a Paragraph   (pages 114–115)

Use the sentences to write a paragraph.

Next, I checked the water with one foot.

Last of all, I jumped in quickly.

First, I walked out to the shore.

Nouns that Name More Than One   (pages 122–127)

Write each noun so that it means more than one.

19. duck   **20.** watch   **21.** berry

22. child   **23.** man   **24.** mouse

Combining Sentences   (pages 130–131)

Write each pair of sentences as one sentence.

25. Mike fixed the kite.
Sue fixed the kite.

26. Mom built a shelf.
I built a shelf.

Composition: Descriptive Paragraph

THE BEACH

Grammar, Mechanics, and Usage: Verbs

USING TOOLS

Practical Language Skills: Vocabulary

TRACK AND FIELD

5

Thinking: Observing

STUDY

Paco is spending the day at the beach. He **sees** the waves. He **hears** the sound they make. He **smells** the fresh air. He **feels** the warm sand. When he splashes in the water, he **tastes** the salty sea.

Paco is using his **five senses** to notice things at the beach. Can you name the five senses?

REMEMBER

> **Seeing, hearing, smelling, touching,** and **tasting** are called the **five senses.**

PRACTICE

Naming the Five Senses Copy these sentences. Next to each one, write the name of the sense that each person is using.

1. Tom listens to the sound of the waves.
2. Pat eats a delicious sandwich.
3. David feels the smooth pebbles.
4. Maria sniffs the fresh air.
5. Laura glimpses a sea gull on a rock.

WRITE

A Chart Copy this chart.

Seeing	Hearing	Smelling	Touching	Tasting

Pretend you are at the beach. List some things you would notice with each of your senses.

Prewriting: A Paragraph That Describes

Last summer, Paco visited Myrtle Beach State Park in South Carolina. He hiked along trails in the forest. He swam at the beach. He liked the beach most of all.

Paco decided to write a paragraph about the beach for the school newspaper. He closed his eyes and pictured the beach in his mind. Then he made a list of things he wanted to describe.

- ✓ A **paragraph that describes** tells about someone or something.
- ✓ Make a list of things you want to describe before you begin writing.

Making a List   Read Paco's list. Copy each thing on the list that you think Paco should describe in his paragraph about the beach.

1. seashells
2. swimming
3. going to a restaurant
4. watching the boats
5. hiking in the woods

A List   Look at the pictures on pages 298–299 in the **DATABANK**. Choose one scene that you would like to write about. Write a list of things you would like to describe.

Writing: A Paragraph That Describes

Paco wanted to describe the beach clearly. He wanted the children in his class to feel as though they had been to Myrtle Beach, too.

He began by writing a sentence that told what the paragraph would be about. Then he added details to describe the beach. Paco used his list to help him in his writing.

Here is Paco's paragraph.

> Myrtle Beach is a beautiful place to visit. The beach is wide and sandy. The water is blue, clear, and warm. Early in the morning, fishing boats move up and down on the gentle waves. The air smells fresh. The seashells along the shore are white, smooth, and shiny.

What are some of the things Paco describes in his paragraph?

148

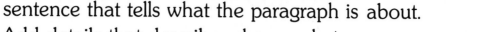

☑ Begin a paragraph that describes with a sentence that tells what the paragraph is about.

☑ Add details that describe who or what you are writing about.

Writing Words That Describe   Copy these words. On each blank, write a word that could be used to describe each thing.

1. ___ sunset
2. ___ air
3. ___ seashells
4. ___ water
5. ___ waves
6. ___ pebbles
7. ___ sand
★ 8. ___ shore

A Paragraph That Describes   Look at the list you made in the last lesson. Use your list to write a paragraph that describes the scene you chose. You can look again at the pictures on pages 298–299 of the **DATABANK** to help you. Remember to begin with a sentence that tells what the paragraph is about. Then add details that describe the scene.

COMPOSITION: Writing/A Paragraph That Describes   **149**

Revising: A Paragraph That Describes

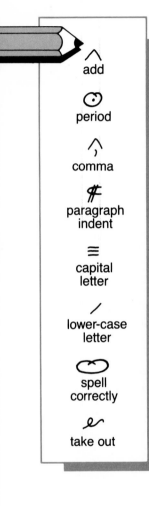

add

period

comma

paragraph indent

capital letter

lower-case letter

spell correctly

take out

Paco's paragraph was not perfect the first time he wrote it. He made some changes in it. Here is the paragraph that Paco wrote at first. Look at the changes in red.

> Myrtle beach is a beautiful place to visit. The beach is wide, and The beach is sandy. The water is blue, clear, and warm. Early in the morning, fishing boats move up and down on the gentle waves. The air smells fresh. The seashells along the shore are white, and smooth, and They are shiny.

Read the second and third sentences before Paco changed them. Both of these sentences describe the beach. Paco combined the two sentences into a longer sentence that describes the beach.

What are the two sentences that Paco combined at the end of his paragraph? What mark of punctuation did Paco add?

Paco also added a word to describe the waves. What word did he use?

Read your paragraph after you have finished writing it. Ask yourself these questions.
- Did I use words that describe things clearly?
- Can I combine short sentences.

Combining Sentences

Read each pair of sentences. Combine each pair of short sentences into a longer sentence.

1. The sun is hot.
   The sun is bright.

2. The air is cool.
   The air is fresh.

3. The sailboats are blue.
   The sailboats are white.

4. The fish were large and striped.
   They were shiny.

Revising a Paragraph That Describes

Copy this paragraph about the Outer Banks in North Carolina. Look for short sentences that can be combined. Try to add a word that describes the wind in the last sentence.

> The Outer Banks are a group of islands off the coast of North Carolina. The islands are small. They are sandy. Sand dunes cover parts of the islands. The sand dunes are smooth. They are large. Winds blow across the islands.

A Revised Paragraph

Read the paragraph you wrote on page 149. Think about ways you can improve it. Use the questions in the **Remember** section on page 150 to help you revise it.

Proofreading: A Paragraph That Describes

STUDY

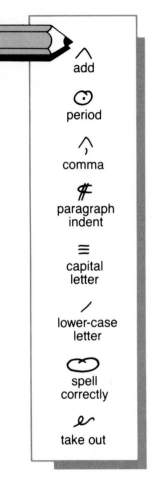

add

period

comma

paragraph indent

capital letter

lower-case letter

spell correctly

take out

You already saw some of the changes Paco made in his paragraph. He made some other changes, too. They are shown in red.

Myrtle beach is a beautiful place to visit. The beach is wide, and The beach is sandy. The water is blue, clear, and warm. Early in the morning, fishing boats move up and down on the gentle waves. The air smells fresh. The seashells along the shore are white, and smooth, and They are shiny.

Look at the third sentence. Paco put in commas after the words *blue* and *clear*.

You need to use commas when you list three or more words in a sentence. What three words are listed?

REMEMBER

Proofread your work. Ask yourself these questions.

- Did I spell everything correctly?
- Did I use capital and small letters correctly?
- Did I use commas correctly?

Adding Commas   Copy these sentences. Add PRACTICE commas where they are needed.

1. I saw seaweed shells and fish.
2. The sunset was red yellow and orange.
3. We ate sandwiches fruit and muffins.
4. The clouds were large soft and white.
5. We swam fished and played at the beach.

Proofreading a Paragraph That Describes

Copy this paragraph. Correct the mistakes in it. Use editing marks to show your corrections.

> Meny people go to California on vacation. They like to visit the clean sandy and beautiful beaches. seals live on some of the beaches. Seals are fun to watch. they swimm dive and play in the ocean. Most seals are friendly and smart.

A Final Copy   Proofread the paragraph you WRITE revised on page 151. Do you see any mistakes in it? Use the questions in the **Remember** section on page 152 as you proofread your work. Write a final copy of your paragraph.

Read the final copy of your paragraph to your SHARE classmates. Ask your classmates to describe beaches, mountains, forests, or deserts they have seen.

Prewrite Choose a topic for your composition project. You may use one of the topics below or choose one of your own.

Write Begin with a sentence that tells what your paragraph is about. Then add details about your topic.

Revise Read your paragraph and try to make it better. Combine short sentences if you can. Make sure you used words that describe things clearly.

Proofread Proofread your paragraph for mistakes in grammar, spelling, and punctuation. Be sure you used capital letters and small letters correctly.

Share Make a neat final copy. Share your paragraph with others.

Social Studies
Look at the picture of harvest festivals on pages 304–305 of the **DATABANK.** Write a paragraph that describes what you see in one of the pictures.

Communications
Listen to the voice of a radio announcer. Imagine what the announcer looks like. Write a paragraph that describes the announcer's voice and what you think the announcer looks like.

Crafts/Hobbies

Think about something that a person in your family or someone else you know made by hand. It could be a quilt, a piece of jewelry, a piece of pottery, or something else. Write a paragraph that describes what the object looks like and feels like.

Health/Physical Education

Have you ever been to a large ballpark to watch a ball game? Write a paragraph that describes the sights and sounds of a ballpark.

Music/Art

Work with a partner. Draw a scene from nature. Have your partner draw a scene, too. Then trade pictures. Write a paragraph describing your partner's picture. Have your partner write a paragraph describing your picture. Then read each other's paragraphs.

Science

Visit a park near your home or school. Notice the trees, flowers, birds, and animals in the park. Then write a paragraph that describes the park.

Forms of *Be*

Not all verbs show action. Some verbs tell about the ways things are. Read the sentences below.

1. I am in a tool store.
2. A hammer is on a shelf.
3. Some nails are in a box.

The verbs *am*, *is*, and *are* are **verbs of being**. They tell about things now. *Am* and *is* are used when the subject names one person, place, or thing. *Are* is used when the subject names more than one. *Are* is also used with *you*.

Read the sentences below.

4. The hammer was heavy.
5. The nails were sharp.

Was and *were* are also verbs of being. They tell about the past. *Was* is used when the subject names one. *Were* is used when the subject names more than one. *Were* is also used with *you*.

REMEMBER

☑ **Verbs of being** tell about the way things are or were.

☑ Use *am*, *is*, and *was* if the subject names one person, place, or thing.

☑ Use *are* and *were* if the subject names more than one.

156

Finding Verbs of Being   Read these sentences.
Write the verb of being in each sentence.

1. I am curious about the tools.
2. The screwdriver is red.
3. The saws are shiny.
4. The tools were new.

⭐ 5. The hammer handle was brown.

Using Verbs of Being   Copy and complete
each sentence. Use the correct word in ( ).

6. This (is, are) Jan's table.
7. Yesterday the table (is, was) in pieces.
8. The table legs (was, were) rough.
9. Today Jan (is, am) busy.
10. Now the table (is, was) almost ready.
11. The table legs (is, are) smooth now.
12. I (am, are) at Jan's house.
13. My friends (is, are) there, too.
⭐ 14. Jan's tools (are, were) new last year.
⭐ 15. Now Jan's tools (are, were) old and used.

A Tool List   Pretend you are building a house
for a pet. Make a list of three of the tools that you
might use. **DATABANK** page 274 will help you.
Write a sentence about each tool on your list. Use
a verb of being in each sentence.

Forms of *Be* + *ing*

Sometimes verbs of being are used with action verbs that end with *-ing*. Verbs of being that are used with action verbs are called **helping verbs**. Read these sentences. Notice the words in color.

1. I am making a salad.
2. Dad is baking bread.
3. We are using bowls and spoons.

The verbs *making*, *baking*, and *using* are action verbs. How does each of these verbs end? Notice that each action verb has a helping verb. What is the helping verb in each sentence?

Am, *is*, and *are* are used with action verbs. Together, these words tell about an action that is happening now. Read these sentences. As you read, ask yourself this question. What are the action verb and helping verb in each sentence?

4. I am peeling carrots.
5. Dad is watching me.
6. We are fixing dinner.

✓ **Helping verbs** are verbs of being that are used with action verbs.

✓ The ending *-ing* is added to an action verb when it is used with a helping verb.

158

Finding Verbs Read these sentences. Copy the
action verb and the helping verb in each sentence.

1. I am cooking dinner.
2. The boys are helping.
3. Jeff is using a mixer.
4. Carl is opening a can.
5. Tom is stirring with a spoon.
6. We are working hard.
7. I am looking for a pan.
8. The boys are peeking into the pots.
⭐ 9. Is the soup cooking?
⭐ 10. Are the potatoes boiling?

Writing Verbs Copy and complete the
sentences. Use one of the action words from the
box in each sentence. Add the helping verb *am*,
is, or *are* to complete the sentence.

| putting | cutting | stirring | cooking |

11. Mom ___ with a knife.
12. I ___ with a spoon.
13. Stan ___ food on a plate.
14. We ___ together.

Sentences Pretend that you and a friend are
making a meal. Write five sentences telling what
you are doing as you make the meal. Use an
action verb with a helping verb in each sentence.

Forms of *Have* and *Do*

Read the sentences below.

1. I have a needle.

2. Joan has some thread.

3. Yesterday we had sewing class.

The verbs *have* and *has* tell about things in the present. *Has* is used when the subject names one person, place, or thing. *Have* is used when the subject names more than one. *Have* is also used with *I* and *you*. *Had* tells about the past.

Now read these sentences.

4. I do my sewing.

5. Pat does her sewing.

6. Yesterday we did our sewing.

The verbs *do* and *does* also tell about things in the present. *Does* is used when the subject names one. *Do* is used when the subject names more than one. *Do* is also used with *I* and *you*. The verb *did* tells about the past.

- ☑ Use *has* and *does* if the subject names one.
- ☑ Use *have* and *do* if the subject names more than one.
- ☑ Use *have* and *do* with *I* and *you*.
- ☑ Use *had* and *did* to tell about the past.

160

Finding Verbs   Copy these sentences. Draw two lines under the verb in each sentence.

1. The children have squares of cloth.
2. José has a pair of scissors.
3. Sara did some cutting.
4. We all do the work.
5. Last year we had a crafts fair.

Choosing Verbs   Copy and complete these sentences. Write the correct verb in (   ).

6. The quilt (have, has) large flowers.
7. Paula (do, does) the cutting.
8. The thread (have, has) a knot in it.
9. The children (has, had) a good time.
10. The needle (have, had) a sharp point.
11. I (have, has) an old pair of scissors.
12. Carla (do, does) her best.
13. Yesterday Sam (does, did) not help.
14. Would you (do, does) that for me?
15. Peter and Kiri (does, did) the sewing.

A Paragraph That Describes   Pretend that your class has made some pillows. Write a paragraph that describes the tools you used. Use a form of the verb *have* in two sentences. Use a form of the verb *do* in two sentences.

Irregular Verbs

STUDY

Many action verbs end in *-ed* when they tell about the past. Some are different. Read the sentences below. Notice the verbs in color.

1. Today we go to the pottery shop.
2. Today Mrs. Jackson goes with us.
3. Yesterday Wendy went to the shop.

Which sentences tell about the present? Which sentence tells about the past? The verbs *go* and *goes* tell about the present. To make the verb *go* tell about the past, you must make a spelling change. The verb *went* tells about the past.

Read the verbs in the box. You must make a spelling change to make them tell about the past.

Present	Past
go, goes	went
see, sees	saw
come, comes	came
run, runs	ran
begin, begins	began
give, gives	gave

REMEMBER

✓ You must make a spelling change to make some action verbs tell about the past.

162

Naming the Tense of a Verb   Copy the underlined verb in each sentence. Decide if the verb tells about something that is happening in the present or something that happened in the past. Write *present* or *past* next to each verb.

1. Yesterday Mr. Scott <u>came</u> to our class.
2. He <u>began</u> to teach us how to work with clay.
3. Today Mr. Scott <u>gives</u> us lessons on how to use tools.
4. Frank <u>sees</u> what Mr. Scott is doing.
5. Judy <u>ran</u> home with the animal she made.
6. She <u>gave</u> the animal to her sister.

Changing Verbs From Present to Past
Change the verb in each sentence from present to past. Copy the new sentence.

7. Jill runs to school.
8. She comes with a new tool.
9. She begins her work.
10. Jill gives the tool to Karen.
★ 11. Mr. Carter sees empty paint jars.
★ 12. Mr. Carter goes to the store.

A Paragraph That Describes   Pretend you are on vacation. Write a short paragraph telling about the vacation. Tell what you saw or did yesterday. Then tell about what you are seeing or doing now. Use four of the verbs from this lesson in your paragraph.

Apostrophe in Contractions

Read these sentences. Notice the words in color.

1. I did not have a paintbrush.

2. I didn't have a paintbrush.

Which word in sentence 2 takes the place of *did not*? The word *didn't* is a short way of writing *did not*. *Didn't* is a **contraction**.

Read these sentences.

3. Those tools are not mine.

4. Those tools aren't mine.

Which word is a contraction? Which two words make up the contraction? *Aren't* is a contraction. It is made from the words *are* and *not*. Notice that when you write the contraction *aren't*, you drop the letter *o* from *not*. You replace the *o* with an **apostrophe** '.

Now read the sentence below. As you read, ask yourself these questions. What contraction is used? Which two words make up the contraction? What letter does the apostrophe replace?

5. I haven't seen the hammer.

☑ A **contraction** is a short way to write two words.

☑ An **apostrophe** ' replaces the dropped letter.

164

Finding Contractions   Read these sentences.
Copy each contraction. Then write the two words
that make up each contraction.

1. The children don't want to leave.
2. They haven't finished painting.
3. The wheels aren't on the car.
4. Jane isn't finished with her plane.
5. Paul didn't pick up his tools.

Forming Contractions   Copy these sentences.
Write a contraction for the underlined words.

6. That tool <u>does not</u> belong to me.
7. Sue <u>had not</u> sanded her toy truck.
8. The paint <u>was not</u> dry yet.
9. Edna <u>did not</u> make a plane.
10. The nails <u>were not</u> very sharp.
11. <u>Do not</u> forget to cover the paint.
12. This hammer <u>is not</u> heavy.
13. Chet <u>has not</u> used the red paint.
⋆ 14. <u>Are</u> the children <u>not</u> ready to leave?
⋆ 15. <u>Have</u> you <u>not</u> used the tools before?

A Letter   Pretend a friend has asked you to
visit his or her classroom. Your friend wants you
to see the toys that the children have made. Write
a letter to your friend saying that you cannot go.
Use at least two contractions in your letter.

Sentence Combining: Predicates

STUDY

Every sentence has a subject and a predicate. When two sentences have the same subject, you can join the predicates.

Read these sentences. Notice the words in color.

1. Meg picked flowers.
2. Meg pressed them.

What is the subject of each sentence? What is the predicate of each sentence?

Subject	Predicate
Meg	picked flowers
	pressed them

You can join the predicates to make a new sentence. Read the new sentence below. Notice that the word *and* joins the two predicates.

3. Meg picked flowers and pressed them.

Now read sentence 4. As you read, ask yourself these questions. What is the subject of the sentence? What two predicates have been joined?

4. Meg opened the book and looked at the flowers.

166

☑ If two sentences have the same subject, the predicates can be joined.

☑ Use *and* to join two predicates.

Finding Sentences With Two Predicates

Read these sentences. Copy only the sentences that have two predicates joined together. Ring the two predicates.

1. The children sit and work.
2. The room is very busy.
3. One girl threads a needle and sews.
4. A boy draws and cuts.

Joining Sentences

Read each pair of sentences. Make a new sentence by joining the two predicates together.

5. Mark cuts.
   Mark folds.
6. Fran hammers.
   Fran saws.
7. Bob makes a drum.
   Bob paints a drum.

☆ 8. Ben braids some cloth.
   Ben makes a rug.

Sentences

Write three sentences about making a craft project. In each sentence, join two predicates with the word *and*.

Legs That Cannot Walk

STUDY

Parts of things often have names that are the same as parts of our bodies. A table stands on its *legs*. A clock points to the time with its *hands*. What do you think the bottom of a bed is called? What do you think the top of a pin is called?

PRACTICE

Describing Things The pictures below show things with body parts instead of their real parts. Write words to describe what is shown in each picture on a piece of paper.

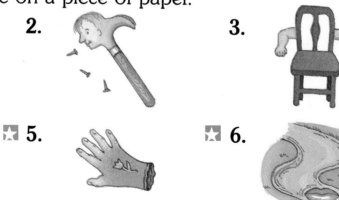

1.

2.

3.

4.

⭐ 5.

⭐ 6.

WRITE

Writing a Paragraph Write a paragraph describing three things in your classroom. Use words such as *arm of, leg of, foot of, hands of,* and *head of* to describe these things.

168 LANGUAGE HISTORY: Metaphoric Extension

Language and Logic

Sentences With *Some*

Look at the picture. Then read sentence 1.

STUDY

1. Some of the tools are hammers.

Sentence 1 is true. In sentence 1, *some* means "a few" or "several." This is the meaning *some* usually has.

Some can also have a special meaning. It can mean "at least one." This is what *some* means in sentence 2.

2. Some of the tools are saws.

Sentence 2 is true.

Now read sentence 3.

3. Some of the tools are drills.

You see that not one of the tools is a drill. You know that *some* means "at least one." So sentence 3 is false.

Using *Some* in Sentences   Study the picture again. Rewrite these sentences. Begin each sentence with *some*.

PRACTICE

1. One of the tools is a wrench.

2. Three of the tools are pliers.

3. Several of the tools are hammers.

4. A few of the tools are screwdrivers.

⭐ **5.** At least one of the tools has teeth.

Prefixes

Read these sentences. Look at the words in color. How are the words alike? How are they different?

1. I was happy when I won the race.

2. Our team was unhappy when we lost.

The letters *un* were added to the word *happy* to make the word *unhappy*.

A **prefix** is a group of letters that is added to the beginning of a word. The prefix *un-* means "not." The prefix *un-* can also mean "opposite of." *Un-* was added to the word *happy.* What does *unhappy* mean?

Read these sentences.

3. It may be unsafe to run so fast.

4. Jane will untie her running shoes.

What does *unsafe* mean? What does *untie* mean?

The prefix *re-* means "again."

5. We had to restart the race.

What does *restart* mean?

Prefix	Meaning	Example
un-	not	unwell
un-	opposite of	unzip
re-	again	relearn

170

✓ A **prefix** is a group of letters added to the beginning of a word.

✓ A prefix changes the meaning of the word.

Finding Prefixes   Copy each sentence.

Underline each word that has a prefix.

1. It was unlucky when Jared slipped.
2. Susan refilled the runners' water jug.
3. Preston's shoe came untied during the race.
4. Preston stopped to retie his shoe.
5. The team was unable to catch up.

Using Prefixes   Copy these sentences. Finish

each one with a word from the box.

unfair	unbroken	undress
rebuilt	reread	

6. We ___ the rules for the race.
7. I thought the rules were ___.
8. The team will ___ in the changing room.
9. The team's record is still ___.
10. We ___ our team when Nancy moved.

Sentences   Write a sentence using each of the

following words. Then add a prefix to each word and write a new sentence for each word.

fair   buttoned   write   do

Suffixes

Read this sentence. Look at the word in color. What letters were added to *hope*?

1. I was hopeful that I would win.

A **suffix** is a group of letters that is added to the end of a word to change its meaning. When a suffix is added to a word, the word is used differently in the sentence. The suffix *-ful* means "full of." What does *hopeful* mean?

Now read this sentence.

2. It is hopeless to try to beat Nora.

The suffix *-less* means "without." What does *hopeless* mean?

The suffix *-er* means "a person who does something." Read this sentence. What does *teacher* mean?

3. Our teacher blew the whistle.

Suffix	Meaning	Example
-ful	full of	cheerful
-less	without	fearless
-er	person who does something	catcher

172

☑ A **suffix** is a group of letters added to the end of a word.

☑ A suffix changes the meaning of the word.

☑ Adding a suffix changes the way a word is used in a sentence.

Finding Suffixes   Copy each sentence. Draw a line under each word that has a suffix.

1. Be careful in the egg and spoon race.
2. Which helper was at the finish line?
3. I was thankful when our team won.
4. You must be fearless to win the three-legged race.
5. That race left me breathless.

★ 6. Which worker set up the obstacle course?

Using Suffixes   Add a suffix to each of these words to make a new word. Then write the meaning of the new word.

7. farm
8. joy
9. sleep
10. power
11. play
12. home
★ 13. sleeve
★ 14. peace

A Poster   Make a poster about a field day at your school. Tell about the races and other games. Use at least four words that have the suffixes *-er, -less,* and *-ful.*

Compound Words

Read this sentence. Look at the word in color. What two smaller words can you find in *football?*

1. I threw the football.

Football is a compound word. A **compound word** is made by putting two words together to make a new word.

Now read this sentence. What is the compound word?

2. We watched from the sidewalk.

What two words are put together to make the compound word?

Find two compound words in this sentence.

3. An airplane flew over the playground.

What two words are put together to make each new word?

A **compound word** is a word made by putting two words together.

174

Finding Compound Words Find the compound word in each list of words. Copy the compound words.

1. basketball   older   dog
2. show   horseshoes   singer
3. sitting   popcorn   light
4. top   reread   baseball
5. outfield   night   careful

Using Compound Words Put together words from row 1 with words from row 2 to make compound words. Use each word only once. Copy the paragraph. Complete it with the compound words you made.

Row 1:	news	head	sun	grand	flag
Row 2:	line	paper	pole	shine	father

      For our field day we ran our school flag up the ___. My ___ came to watch the games. He said it was hot in the ___. I won the most prizes. The next day the ___ in the ___ was "Girl Wins Six Blue Ribbons."

How-to Paragraph Read the paragraph about football on page 277 of the **DATABANK.** Think of a compound word that names another game. You might think of baseball or leapfrog. Write a paragraph telling about the game. Underline all the compound words you use.

Composition   Write a short paragraph that describes your favorite toy.

Grammar, Mechanics, and Usage   Choose the correct way to write each sentence.

1. (a) Ed joe, and Kim ran.   (b) ed, Joe and, Kim ran.
   (c) Ed, Joe, and Kim ran.   (d) Ed Joe and Kim ran.

2. (a) I saw pigs, sheep and   (b) I saw pigs, sheep, and
       goats, at the farm.   goats at the farm.
   (c) I saw pigs sheep and   (d) I saw pigs, sheep and
       goats at the farm.   goats at the farm.

Choose the correct verb to complete each sentence.

3. The dog __ brown.   4. The trees __ tall.
   (a) am   (b) is   (a) is   (b) are

5. Those shoes __ old.   6. I __ at the game last week.
   (a) was   (b) were   (a) is   (b) was

7. I am __ Mom.   8. We are __ crayons.
   (a) help (b) helping   (a) using (b) used

9. Now I __ a book.   10. I __ a cold last week.
   (a) have (b) has   (a) has   (b) had

Choose the correct word to complete each sentence.

11. I __ my work now.   12. I __ the job already.
    (a) do   (b) did   (a) does (b) did

13. Now Meg ___ home
   ⓐ go   ⓑ goes

14. We ___ again last week.
   ⓐ go   ⓑ went

15. I ___ Ed last week.
   ⓐ sees ⓑ saw

16. We ___ yesterday.
   ⓐ run ⓑ ran

Choose the word that is made from the underlined words.

17. I <u>do not</u> have a book.
   ⓐ didn't ⓑ don't

18. He <u>had not</u> helped me.
   ⓐ hadn't   ⓑ hasn't

19. Henry <u>is not</u> playing.
   ⓐ aren't ⓑ isn't

20. Jan <u>was not</u> at the park.
   ⓐ weren't   ⓑ wasn't

Choose the sentences from which the example was made.

21. Pat sang and danced.
   ⓐ Pat sang. Jan sang.   ⓑ Pat sang. I danced.
   ⓒ Pat sang. Pat danced.   ⓓ Pat sang. We danced.

Practical Language Skills Choose the word that means the same as the underlined words.

22. I <u>tied</u> my shoes <u>again</u>.
   ⓐ untied ⓑ retied

23. The meat is <u>not cooked</u>.
   ⓐ uncooked ⓑ recooked

Choose the compound word.

24. <u>The</u> <u>sunset</u> <u>is</u> <u>lovely</u>.
   ⓐ ⓑ ⓒ ⓓ

25. <u>I</u> <u>rebuilt</u> <u>the</u> <u>doghouse</u>.
   ⓐ ⓑ ⓒ ⓓ

Composition: How-To Paragraph

INSTRUMENTS

Grammar, Mechanics, and Usage: Pronouns

THE TELEPHONE

Practical Language Skills: Study Skills

AT THE LIBRARY

178

Thinking: Generalizing

STUDY

Ken wants to buy a guitar. He goes to Melodyland music store to look at guitars on sale. They are all made of wood. Which sentence is correct?

1. All guitars are made of wood.
2. All guitars at Melodyland are made of wood.
3. All guitars made of wood are on sale at Melodyland.

REMEMBER

☑ When you **generalize**, you make a statement about all the members of a group.

☑ Be sure that your generalization is true for *all* the members in the group.

PRACTICE

Thinking About Generalizations Read each sentence. Think about it carefully. Write *true* or *false* next to each generalization.

1. All guitars have strings.
2. All guitars are made of metal.
3. All adults can play the guitar.
4. All guitars are made of parts.

WRITE

Sentences Write two generalizations about drums. Make one of them true. Make the other one false. Begin both sentences with *All*.

Prewriting:
A How-To Paragraph

Stu likes the flowerpot bells Rita made. Stu asks Rita how to make them. First, Rita tells Stu what things she used. Then she tells him the steps she followed.

STUDY

✔ A **how-to paragraph** tells how to do something or how to make something.

✔ A how-to paragraph tells what things are needed and what steps to follow.

REMEMBER

Writing Steps in Order   These sentences are steps from a how-to paragraph about making a flowerpot bell. Write the steps in the correct order.

PRACTICE

1. Second, tie the end of the string to the stick.
2. First, you need a flowerpot, a long string, a small stick, and a pencil.
3. Last of all, hold the flowerpot by the string and hit it with the pencil.
4. Next, put the other end of the string through the hole in the flowerpot and knot the string.

Lists   Read the article on page 294 in the **DATABANK**. Pretend that you are going to make a musical instrument. Make a list of the things you will need. Then list the steps to follow.

WRITE

Writing: A How-To Paragraph

Taro made a drum. Now Brian wants to make one. Taro writes this paragraph to help Brian make a drum.

> You can use a pail to make a drum. First, you need a metal pail, a piece of cloth or plastic, and string. Second, fill the pail with water until it is about one-third full. Third, tie the cloth or plastic tightly over the pail with the string. Play the drum with your fingers or a stick.

Taro's first sentence tells what the paragraph is about. His next sentence lists the items Brian will need.

Taro used signal words such as *first* and *second*. **Signal words** show the order in which things are done. What other signal word did Taro use in his how-to paragraph?

- ☑ Begin a how-to paragraph with a sentence that *tells* what the paragraph is about.
- ☑ Tell the materials that are needed.
- ☑ Use signal words such as *first, second, third, next*, and *last* in the paragraph.

182

Sequencing a How-To Paragraph   The sentences below tell how to make a drumstick. Put the sentences in order. Then write a how-to paragraph with a sentence that tells what the paragraph is about.

1. Last, let the glue dry before using the drumstick.

2. First, find an empty thread spool, a pencil or a chopstick, and some glue.

3. Next, put that end of the pencil or chopstick into the hole in the spool.

4. Second, put some glue on the writing end of the pencil or on the end of the chopstick.

Completing a How-To Paragraph   Copy this paragraph. Write a sentence that tells what the paragraph is about. Add signal words.

_____

_____. First, you will need a paper towel tube and some crayons or paints. ____, decorate the tube with music notes. ____, put your mouth to the tube and toot a tune.

A How-To Paragraph   Write a paragraph telling how to make a musical instrument. Use the lists you wrote for the **Write** activity on page 181. Begin with a sentence that tells what the paragraph is about. In the next sentence, list the materials that are needed. Use signal words in your paragraph.

Revising:
A How-To Paragraph

STUDY

When Taro wrote his paragraph the first time, he had to make some changes. This is how it looked.

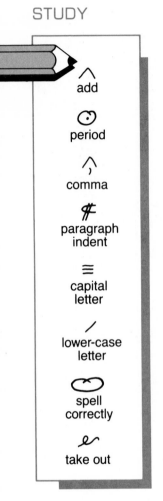

add

period

comma

paragraph
indent

capital
letter

lower-case
letter

spell
correctly

take out

You can use a pail to make a drum.

First, you need a metal pail, a piece of cloth or plastic, and string. Second, Fill the pail with water until it is about one-third full. third. tie the cloth or plastic tightly over the pail with the string. Play the drum with your fingers or a stick.

Taro knew he needed a sentence to tell what the paragraph was about. He also added a signal word to help show the order of the steps.

REMEMBER

Read through your how-to paragraph. Ask yourself these questions.
- Did I write a sentence that tells what the paragraph is about?
- Are the steps in the correct order?
- Do I need signal words to show the order of the steps?

Combining Sentences   Read these
sentences. Then combine each pair and write the
new sentence.

1. Making musical instruments can be easy.
   Making musical instruments can be fun.

2. Pot lids can be cymbals.
   Pie tins can be cymbals.

3. Cymbals are loud.
   Drums are loud.

4. I can make many musical instruments.
   I can play many musical instruments.

Revising a How-To Paragraph   Write the
sentences in this paragraph in order. Add the
signal words *first, second, third*. Then join the last
two sentences.

You can make a kazoo out of a comb.
You find a comb and a piece of wax paper.
You put the teeth of the comb in the fold of
the paper. You fold the paper in half. Last,
you put your lips over the paper. You hum a
tune.

A Revised How-To Paragraph   Read the
paragraph you wrote for the **Write** activity on
page 183. Does your paragraph tell all the
important facts in order? Can you join any of
these sentences or add signal words? Change
anything you need to.

Proofreading:
A How-To Paragraph

Taro read his paragraph again. This time he checked his spelling. He also made sure he used capital letters and periods correctly.

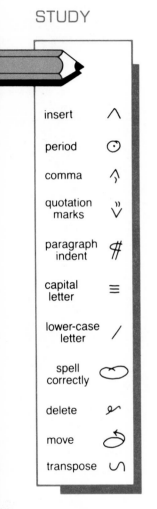

insert — ∧

period — ⊙

comma — ⌄

quotation marks — ˅

paragraph indent — ⌗

capital letter — ≡

lower-case letter — /

spell correctly — ⌒

delete — ℒ

move — ↻

transpose — ∽

You can use a pail to make a drum⊙

∧First, you need a metal pail⌄ a piece of cloth or plastic⌄ and string. ∧Fill the pail with water until it is about one-third full. third, ⊙tie⊙ly⊙ the cloth or plastic tightly over the pail with the string⊙ Play the drum with ⊙your⊙ fingers or a stick.

Taro had forgotten to put commas between the three materials he listed. These commas help to make a list in a sentence easier to read.

◪ Read your how-to paragraph again. Ask yourself these questions.

- Did I use capital letters and periods correctly?
- Did I spell all the words correctly?
- Did I put a comma between three or more words in a list?

Proofreading Sentences   Copy these sentences. Use editing marks to show your corrections. Correct any spelling mistakes.

1. first, you will need a shoo box a string and some nails.

2. you will need two blocks of would some sandpaper and some glue.

3. first, take out a mixing bowl a piece of cloth and some string.

Proofreading a How-To Paragraph   Copy this paragraph. Use editing marks to correct it.

here is how to make castanets out of a walnut. First, you need a large walnut a nutcracker and some tape. Second, you krack the walnut in half with the nutcracker and empty the shell Third, you tape one haff of the shell to your thumb and the other Half to your pointing finger. last, click your thumb and finger together to play.

A Final Copy   Read the paragraph you wrote for the **Write** activity on page 185. Correct the paragraph if you need to. Then write a neat, final copy.

Read your final how-to paragraph to a friend. Then ask your friend to try to make the instrument you described in your paragraph.

Composition Projects

Prewrite   Choose a topic for your composition project. You may use one of the topics below or choose one of your own. Begin by making a list or talking to other people.

Write   Begin your how-to paragraph by putting your ideas on paper. Be sure your paragraph explains things clearly. Remember to use signal words.

Revise   Read your paragraph and try to make it better. Check to be sure that the steps are in the correct order. Combine sentences if you can, and add signal words if you need to.

Proofread   Read your paragraph again. Proofread it for errors in spelling and grammar. Make sure you used capital letters, commas, and periods correctly. Also, check to be sure your handwriting is clear.

Share   Share your writing with others.

Health/Physical Education
Read pages 278–279 in the **DATABANK**. They tell about a picnic game. Then write a paragraph that explains how to play that game or another outdoor game that you like.

Communications

Write a paragraph that tells how to use the telephone to get help in an emergency. Be sure to tell the correct telephone numbers and the kind of information you would have to give.

Crafts

Many recipes can be written as how-to paragraphs. Write a paragraph that explains how to make a meal or a snack that you enjoy. Share your recipe with other children in your class.

Literature

Write a story in which one person tells another how to do something. Have the second person ask one or two questions. The questions should help him or her understand the explanation.

Mathematics

Write a paragraph telling how to use a pocket calculator. Explain how to do an addition or subtraction example on the calculator.

Social Studies

Write a paragraph explaining how a friend can get from school to your home. Be sure to give the names of the streets along the way. Describe anything important that your friend should notice on the way to your home.

Understanding Pronouns

A **pronoun** is a word that takes the place of a noun. Read these sentences. Notice the word in color.

1. Mr. Bell worked hard.
2. He listened closely.

What is the noun in sentence 1? What word in sentence 2 takes the place of *Mr. Bell*? The pronoun *he* takes the place of the noun *Mr. Bell*.

Pronouns add interest to sentences. You can use a pronoun instead of using the same noun again and again.

Read the words in the box. These words are pronouns that are often used in sentences.

| I | we | you | he | she | it | they | us |

Read the sentences below. As you read, ask yourself these questions. What pronoun takes the place of *people*? What pronoun takes the place of *telephone*?

3. People like the telephone.
4. They use it.

☑ A **pronoun** takes the place of a noun.

☑ Pronouns add interest to sentences.

Finding Pronouns   Copy these sentences.
Draw a line under the pronouns.

1. Alexander Graham Bell gave us the telephone.
2. He was working with a telegraph.
3. It could send many messages.
4. We know what happened next.
5. Mr. Bell thought of it.
6. He asked Thomas Watson to help.
7. They worked as a team.
8. One day they heard voices over the wire.
9. You and I are lucky.
10. They gave us the telephone.

Finding Pronouns and the Nouns They Replace   Copy each pair of sentences. Draw a line under the pronoun. Ring the noun that the pronoun replaces.

11. Mr. Bell worked hard. He didn't give up.
12. Mrs. Bell helped. She liked Mr. Bell's idea.
13. Mr. Watson helped. He knew about wires.
14. Mr. Bell talked to people. They listened.
15. Telephones would soon be coming. They would change the world.

A Message   Pretend that you are Mr. Bell. You
want to send the first telephone message. Write three sentences. Use pronouns in two sentences.

Subject Pronouns

Pronouns that are used in the subject are called **subject pronouns.** Read these sentences. Notice the words in color.

1. Dan went to the store. He saw a red telephone.

2. Cora and Sue tried a new telephone. They liked the new phones.

Who saw a red telephone? What noun does the pronoun *he* replace? *Dan* names one person. The pronoun *he* is a **singular pronoun.**

Who liked the new phones? What two nouns does the pronoun *they* replace? *Cora* and *Sue* name two people. The pronoun *they* is a **plural pronoun.**

Read the words in the boxes. They are singular and plural subject pronouns.

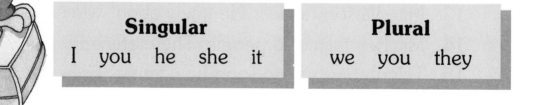

Singular					Plural		
I	you	he	she	it	we	you	they

☑ **Subject pronouns** are often used in the subject of a sentence.

☑ Subject pronouns have **singular** and **plural** forms.

192

Finding Singular and Plural Pronouns

Read these sentences. Write the subject pronoun.
Then write *singular* if the pronoun names one.
Write *plural* if the pronoun names more than one.

1. We like to visit the telephone store.
2. They sell many kinds of telephones.
3. He listens to the musical telephone.
4. It rings four times.
5. She buys a blue telephone.
6. It lights up in the dark.
★ 7. You should see the dinosaur telephone.
★ 8. She and I tried several telephones.

Writing Pronouns   Copy and complete the
paragraph. Use each pronoun only once.

he	it	she	we	I

Jill has a new telephone. ___ is yellow. ___
am visiting Jill to see the new telephone. Jill
pushes seven buttons. ___ calls her friend, Ken.
The telephone rings in Ken's house. ___ answers
the telephone. Jill's brothers and I gather around
the telephone. ___ can hear Ken's voice.

A Paragraph That Explains   Pretend that
you meet someone who has never used a
telephone. Write a paragraph that explains how to
make a telephone call. Use a subject pronoun in
three sentences.

Object Pronouns

STUDY

A pronoun is often used in the predicate of a sentence after an action verb. These pronouns are called **object pronouns.** Read these sentences.

1. Rosa spoke to Mr. Garcia. Rosa asked him for two phone numbers.

2. Mr. Garcia gave them to Rosa.

Whom did Rosa ask for two phone numbers? What noun does *him* replace? *Mr. Garcia* names one person. *Him* is a singular pronoun.

What did Mr. Garcia give to Rosa? The pronoun *them* replaces *phone numbers. Them* is a plural pronoun.

Read the words in the boxes. They are singular and plural object pronouns.

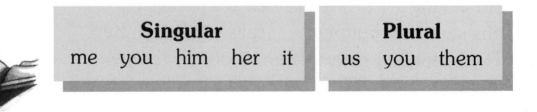

Singular					**Plural**		
me	you	him	her	it	us	you	them

REMEMBER

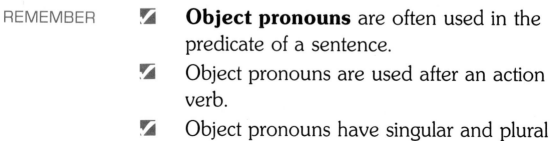

- ✓ **Object pronouns** are often used in the predicate of a sentence.
- ✓ Object pronouns are used after an action verb.
- ✓ Object pronouns have singular and plural forms.

194

Finding Singular and Plural Pronouns

Read these sentences. Write the object pronoun that comes after the action verb. Write *singular* if the pronoun names one. Write *plural* if the pronoun names more than one.

1. Mr. Smith's dogs love him.
2. Mr. Smith cannot find them.
3. Mr. Smith calls us on the telephone.
4. Mother picks it up.
★ 5. Mr. Smith tells her about the dogs.
★ 6. Mr. Smith asks you and me to help.

Writing Pronouns   Read each sentence. Think of a pronoun to take the place of the underlined nouns. Then write each sentence using the pronoun. Use each pronoun from the box only once.

us	her	him	them

7. Jill calls <u>Ken</u> every day.
8. Ken helps <u>Jill</u> with spelling.
★ 9. The telephone helps <u>Jill and Ken</u>.
★ 10. The telephone can help <u>Sam and me</u>, too.

Sentences   Write five sentences that tell how airport workers get facts to use in their work. **DATABANK** pages 302–303 will tell you many facts about airports.

Correct Usage of *I* and *Me*

You can use pronouns to talk about yourself.

Read these sentences. Notice the words in color.

1. Sandy called me.

2. I answered the telephone.

Whom did Sandy call? Who answered the telephone? The pronoun *me* is used in the predicate of the sentence. The pronoun *I* is used in the subject of the sentence. Notice that the word *I* is always a capital letter.

Read these sentences.

3. Sandy and I made a plan.

4. Sandy will meet with Ken and me.

What pronoun is used in each sentence? The pronouns *I* and *me* take the place of your name. Always name yourself last.

☑ Use the pronoun *I* in the subject of a sentence.

☑ Use the pronoun *me* in the predicate of a sentence.

☑ Write the word *I* as a capital letter.

☑ Always name yourself last.

196

Finding Pronouns   Read these sentences.
Write the pronoun. Tell whether the pronoun is
used in the subject or the predicate of the sentence.

1. I have a new telephone.
2. Mom shows me how to use the
   telephone.
3. I can see the person on the other end.
4. The person sees me, too.
5. Dad shows me another telephone.
6. I do not need to push seven buttons.
7. Dad tells me to push one button.
8. Then I can speak.
★ 9. Mr. King will show Dad and me more
   telephones.
★ 10. Dad and I like the new telephones.

Using *I* and *Me* Correctly   Copy and
complete these sentences. Write *I* or *me.*

11. Mary and ___call each other every day.
12. Mary helps ___with spelling.
13. Mary reads ___the words on the list.
14. ___write the words.
15. The telephone helps
    Mary and ___ .

A Funny Story   Write a funny story about a
telephone call you received. Tell what happened.
Use the pronouns *I* and *me* in your story.

Language Play

Telephone Codes

STUDY

Many telephones have letters and numbers on their dials. Some telephones have letters and numbers on their buttons. Look at the telephone above. Which letters appear over the number 2? Which letters appear over the number 8?

PRACTICE

Figuring Out Telephone Codes   Read the telephone codes and the clues below. Find each number in the code on the telephone. Write each set of letters above the number on a piece of paper. Choose one letter from each set to make a word to fit the clue. Then write the word you make.

Telephone Codes	Clues
1. 228	an animal that makes a nice pet
2. 726	went faster than walking
3. 534	body part on which a person stands
★ 4. 866	the weight of something very heavy
★ 5. 929	what bees use to make their honeycomb

WRITE

Writing a Message   Use a telephone code to write a message to a friend in your class. Then ask your friend to find the meaning of the message. Give your friend clues to the words if necessary.

Language and Logic

More About *All, None,* and *Some*

Look at the picture. Then read sentences 1–3.

1. Every telephone in the picture has a cord.
2. No telephone in the picture is black.
3. Several of the telephones have dials.

Sentences 1–3 could be written in another way. They could include *all, none,* and *some.* Read sentences 4–6.

4. All of the telephones in the picture have cords.
5. None of the telephones in the picture are black.
6. Some of the telephones have dials.

Look at sentences 1 and 4. *Every* and *all* have almost the same meaning. Look at sentences 2 and 5. *No* and *none* have nearly the same meaning. Look at sentences 3 and 6. *Several* and *some* have nearly the same meaning.

Using *All, None,* and *Some* in Sentences

Rewrite each sentence. Use *all, none,* or *some* at the beginning.

1. Every telephone is on sale.
2. No telephone costs more than $100.
3. A few telephones work on batteries.
 4. Each of the telephones is new.

Parts of a Book

STUDY

Some parts of a book tell you important facts about the book. The **title** is the name of the book. The **author** is the person who wrote the book. Compare this **book jacket** and **title page**.

FUN WITH PETS
by Roger Marin

pictures by
Louise Talbot

FUN WITH PETS
by Roger Marin

pictures by Louise Talbot

Do the book jacket and title page tell the same facts? What is the title of the book? Who is the author? Who drew the pictures?

Some parts of a book tell what is inside the book. Look at these pages.

Contents

		Page
chapter 1	Choosing a Pet	1
chapter 2	Taking Your Pet Home	10
chapter 3	Feeding Your Pet	15
chapter 4	Health and Grooming	21

Index

bedding 11, 13
dogs 4–6
fish 8
food 15–20

The **table of contents** is in the front of the book. It lists the chapter titles and the page where each chapter begins. Where does chapter 4 begin?

200

The **index** is in the back of the book. It lists topics in the book and the pages where each can be found. Is the index in ABC order?

☑ The **book jacket** and **title page** tell the title and author of the book.

☑ The **table of contents** lists the chapter titles and the page number where each begins.

☑ The **index** is a list in ABC order of the topics in the book and where they can be found.

Identifying Parts of a Book   Write *Yes* if the sentence is true. Write *No* if it is not true.

1. The book jacket and title page tell the same facts.

2. The author is the name of the book.

3. The index is in ABC order.

⭐ 4. The table of contents is in the back of the book.

Using Parts of a Book   Write *where* you would find each fact.

5. author's name

6. name of the person who drew the pictures

7. titles of chapters

⭐ 8. how many pages are about food

A List   Choose a book in the school library that has a table of contents and an index. Write three facts found in each part of the book.

Using the Library

STUDY

Read the titles of these books.

Fifty Fairy Tales
How to Train a Dog

Which book is about something real? Books about real people, places, and things are called **nonfiction.** Books about make-believe topics are called **fiction.** *Fifty Fairy Tales* is fiction.

Fiction books and nonfiction books are kept on different shelves in the library. Fiction books are put in ABC order using the author's last name. These fiction books are in ABC order.

Freddy the Detective by Walter R. Brooks
The Snowman by Jim Erskine
The Wonderful Pumpkin by Len Hellsing

Where would a book by Beverly Cleary go in this list?

REMEMBER

- ☑ **Nonfiction** books are about real people, places, and things.
- ☑ **Fiction** books are about make-believe things.
- ☑ In a library, fiction books are put in ABC order by the author's last name.

Identifying Fiction and Nonfiction Write
whether each book is *fiction* or *nonfiction.*

1. *All About Cats*
2. *The Magic Clock*
3. *Planes*
4. *Little Rabbit Goes to School*
5. *Planets and Stars*

Arranging Books in ABC Order Copy the
authors and titles of these fiction books. Then
write them in the order in which they would
appear on a library shelf.

6. *The Snowy Day* by Ezra Jack Keats
7. *Lost in the Storm* by Carol Carrick
8. *Louis the Fish* by Arthur Yorinks
9. *The Sea of Gold* by Yoshiko Uchida
10. *What Mary Jo Shared* by Janice May Udry

A Chart Copy the chart below. Then read
through the **DATABANK** selections. Choose two
selections that are fiction and two that are
nonfiction. Write their titles on your chart.

Fiction	Nonfiction

Filling Out Forms

Pedro had to fill out this **form** to get a library card. First he read it carefully. Then he filled it in. Read the form to see how he filled it in.

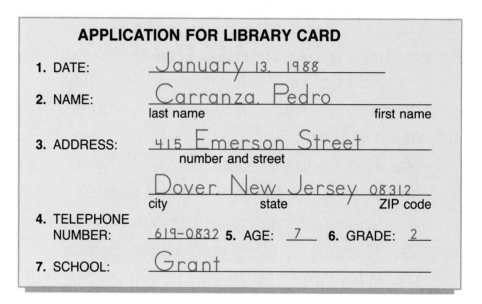

APPLICATION FOR LIBRARY CARD

1. DATE: January 13, 1988

2. NAME: Carranza, Pedro
last name   first name

3. ADDRESS: 415 Emerson Street
number and street

Dover, New Jersey 08312
city   state   ZIP code

4. TELEPHONE NUMBER: 619-0832 **5.** AGE: 7 **6.** GRADE: 2

7. SCHOOL: Grant

You must put information in the right places on a form. Where did Pedro write his name? How did he write it? Where did he write his age?

Pedro printed clearly. When he was done, he checked the form to be sure it was correct. Check his form. Did Pedro forget anything?

- ✓ Read a form carefully.
- ✓ Put information in the right places.
- ✓ Print clearly.
- ✓ Check the information to be sure it is correct.

Reading a Form   Read the form on page 204.
Write the answer to each question.

   1. In what grade is Pedro?
   2. Where does Pedro go to school?
   3. How old is Pedro?
   4. What is Pedro's full name?
⭐ 5. What is Pedro's ZIP code?

Filling Out a Form   Read the form on page
204. Write the answer to each question.

   6. Where do you write the date?
   7. Where do you write your telephone
      number?
   8. How would Judy Brown write her name
      on the form?
⭐ 9. What goes on the first line of item 3?
⭐ 10. What goes on the second line of item 3?

A Form   Pretend that you must fill out a form to
get a library card. Copy the form on page 204.
Fill in the correct information.

Composition   Write a short paragraph that tells how to get from your home to a place in your neighborhood. You might write about a store, the library, the post office, or the firehouse.

Grammar, Mechanics, and Usage   Choose the correct way to write each sentence.

1. (a) The flag is red, white, and blue.
   (b) The flag is, red, white and blue.

2. (a) I live in Ames, Iowa.
   (b) I live in Ames Iowa.

3. (a) It is May, 9, 1988.
   (b) It is May 9, 1988.

Choose the word that can take the place of the underlined word or words.

4. <u>Gail</u> will speak next.
   (a) He   (b) She

5. <u>The table</u> is dusty.
   (a) She   (b) It

6. <u>The children</u> read.
   (a) We   (b) They

7. <u>Ben and I</u> fly kites.
   (a) We   (b) They

8. Please give it to <u>Ann</u>.
   (a) him   (b) her

9. Tom likes <u>you and me</u>.
   (a) us   (b) them

Choose the correct way to write each sentence.

10. (a) Jeff and me are busy.
    (b) Me and Jeff are busy.
    (c) I and Jeff are busy.
    (d) Jeff and I are busy.

11.
   ⓐ Bob sees me and Meg.   ⓑ Bob sees Meg and me.
   ⓒ Bob sees Meg and I.   ⓓ Bob sees I and Meg.
12.
   ⓐ Pat, Al, and I will go.   ⓑ Pat, me, and Al will go.
   ⓒ I, Pat, and Al will go.   ⓓ Pat, Al, and me will go.

Practical Language Skills Read the book cover and the table of contents. Then choose the correct answer.

Hiking in the Woods

by Robert James

Pictures by Sue Green

CONTENTS

		Page
CHAPTER 1	What to Wear	2
CHAPTER 2	Where to Hike	10
CHAPTER 3	Where to Camp	25

13. Who is the author of the book?
   ⓐ <u>Hiking in the Woods</u> ⓑ Robert James ⓒ Sue Green
14. What is the title of the book?
   ⓐ <u>Hiking in the Woods</u> ⓑ Robert James ⓒ Sue Green
15. Which chapter begins on page 10?
   ⓐ Chapter 1   ⓑ Chapter 2   ⓒ Chapter 3
16. What is Chapter 3 about?
   ⓐ Things to wear ⓑ Places to hike ⓒ Places to camp

Choose whether each book is fiction or nonfiction.

17. <u>The Dog from Outer Space</u>   18. <u>How to Train a Dog</u>
   ⓐ fiction ⓑ nonfiction   ⓐ fiction ⓑ nonfiction
19. <u>All About Trains</u>   20. <u>Rabbit's Birthday</u>
   ⓐ fiction ⓑ nonfiction   ⓐ fiction ⓑ nonfiction

Composition:
A Book Report

FOLK AND FAIRY TALES

Grammar, Mechanics, and Usage:
Adjectives and Adverbs

COUNTRIES AROUND THE WORLD

Practical Language Skills:
Critical Reading Skills

IN THE MATH CLASS

Reading a Schedule, a Graph, and a Flowchart

Thinking: Cause and Effect

Think about the story of *The Three Little Pigs*. What happened to the straw house that one of the pigs built? What caused this to happen?

☑ A **cause** tells why something happened.
☑ An **effect** tells what happened.

Telling the Cause or the Effect   Look at the pictures. Then write an answer to each question.

1. Why did Humpty Dumpty break?
2. Why did Baby Bear's chair break?
3. Why did the man take his coat off?

Sentences   Think about a story you know. Write a sentence that tells about something that happens in the story. Then write another sentence that tells what caused this to happen.

210

Prewriting: Book Report

Angela is going to write a book report about a book called *Anansi the Spider*. Before she writes the book report, she asks herself these questions.

1. What is the title of the book?
2. Who is the author?
3. Whom or what is the book about?
4. What are two things that happen?
5. Do I like the book? Why or why not?

- A **book report** is a paragraph that tells important information about a book.
- Before you write a book report, ask yourself some questions about the book.

Prewriting a Book Report Read the book *The Magic Porridge Pot* on **DATABANK** pages 280–283. Copy **Study** questions 1–5. Use the book to answer the **Study** questions.

Sentences Choose a book that you like. Ask yourself questions 1–5 in **Study**. Write sentences to answer the questions.

Writing: Book Report

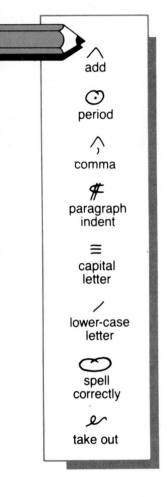

add

period

comma

paragraph
indent

capital
letter

lower-case
letter

spell
correctly

take out

Angela thinks about the five questions she asked herself about *Anansi the Spider*. Then she writes this book report.

I read a book called <u>Anansi the Spider</u> by Gerald McDermott. It is about a spider named Anansi and his six sons. Anansi's sons learn that Anansi is in trouble and go to help him. Then Anansi has to decide which son deserves a prize. I liked the book because it showed sons helping their father. I also liked it because Anansi is funny.

What important facts does Angela's book report tell about *Anansi the Spider*?

- ✓ A book report tells the **title** and the **author** of the book.
- ✓ A book report tells **whom** or **what** the book is about and **what happened**.
- ✓ A book report tells **why** you liked or did not like the book.

Answering Questions About a Book

Look at Angela's book report about *Anansi the Spider*. Then write the answers to these questions about the book.

1. What is the title of the book?
2. Who is the author?
3. Whom or what is the book about?
4. What are two things that happen?
5. Why did Angela like the book?

Completing a Book Report Think about the book *The Magic Porridge Pot*. Copy this paragraph. Look back at the **Practice** on page 211. Use it to fill in the blanks.

I read a book called ____by ____. The book is about ____. Two things that happen in the book are ____. I liked the book because ____.

A Book Report Write a book report about the book you chose on page 211. Use the sentences you wrote in the last lesson to help you write the report.

Revising: Book Report

STUDY

Angela's book report was not perfect the first time she wrote it. Here is what Angela wrote at first.

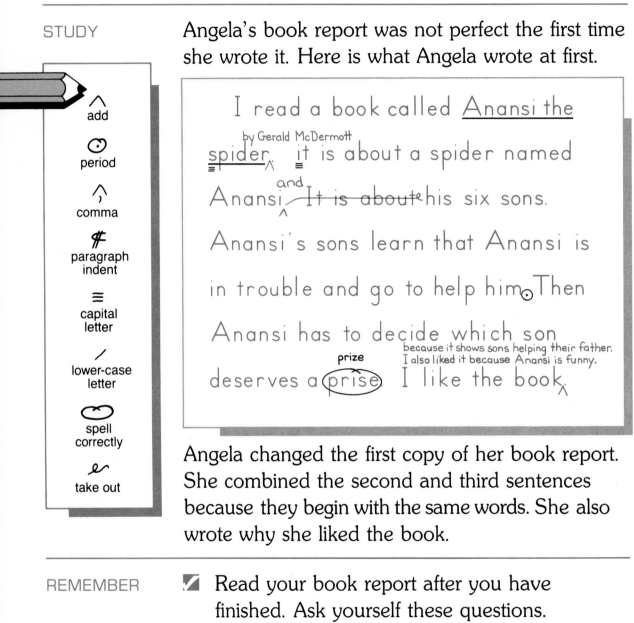

add

period

comma

paragraph indent

capital letter

lower-case letter

spell correctly

take out

Angela changed the first copy of her book report. She combined the second and third sentences because they begin with the same words. She also wrote why she liked the book.

REMEMBER

✓ Read your book report after you have finished. Ask yourself these questions.

- Did I include all important information?
- Did I tell why I liked or did not like the book?
- Can I combine any short sentences?

214

Combining Sentences   Combine each pair of sentences.

1. The wolf huffed and puffed.
   The wolf blew down the straw house.
2. The shoemaker surprised the elves.
   His wife surprised the elves.
3. The bears left their house.
   The bears went for a walk in the woods.
4. The cat would not help the little red hen.
   The dog would not help the little red hen.
5. The beanstalk grew very high.
   The beanstalk touched the sky.

Revising a Book Report   Copy this book report about *The Magic Porridge Pot*. Combine two sentences if you can. Add a reason why a person would like the book. Use a reason that is different from the reasons you used on page 213.

> I enjoyed reading *The Magic Porridge Pot*. The book was written by Paul Galdone. It is about a magic pot. The pot makes porridge for the little girl. The pot makes porridge for her mother. One day the pot will not stop making porridge. I liked the book.

A Revised Book Report   Look at the book report you wrote on page 213. If you did not write sentences telling why you liked the book, add them. Combine sentences in your book report if you can.

Proofreading: Book Report

STUDY

Angela checked her book report again. She noticed that she had made some mistakes. Angela had forgotten to underline the title of the book. She had not used capital letters correctly. Notice how Angela marked her corrections.

∧
add

⊙
period

∧
comma

#
paragraph
indent

≡
capital
letter

/
lower-case
letter

⟳
spell
correctly

✎
take out

I read a book called <u>Anansi the</u>

<u>spider</u>. it is about a spider named   *by Gerald McDermott*

Anansi, <s>It is about</s> his six sons.   *and*

Anansi's sons learn that Anansi is

in trouble and go to help him. Then

Anansi has to decide which son

deserves a (prise). I like the book.   *prize*   *because it shows sons helping their father.*
                                                      I also liked it because Anansi is funny.

Important words in the title begin with capital letters.

REMEMBER

◪ Proofread your work. Ask yourself these questions.
- Did I spell everything correctly?
- Did I use capital and small letters correctly?
- Did I use commas and periods correctly?

Correcting Book Titles   Copy these titles. PRACTICE
Use editing marks to correct them.

1. *the Monkey's whiskers*
2. *stone soup*
3. *the angry Moon*
4. *Arrow To The Sun*

5. *how Tevye Became A Milkman*

Proofreading a Book Report   Copy this
book report. Use editing marks to correct it.

I enjoyed reading a book called
Madeline's rescue by Ludwig Bemelmans. the
book is about a little girl named Madeline
She falls into a rivver. A dog saves her. The
dog comes to live with Madeline but then
runz away. I liked the book because the dog
was brave. I also liked the surprise ending.

A Final Copy   Read the book report you wrote   WRITE
on page 215. Did you draw a line under the title
of the book? Did you use capital letters correctly?
Correct your book report if you need to.

Read your final book report to your class. Ask   SHARE
your classmates if they think the book would be
interesting to read.

Prewrite   Choose a topic for your composition project. You may use one of the topics below or choose one of your own. Ask yourself some questions about the book.

Write   Think about the book you have read and write your report. Be sure to tell why you did or did not like the book.

Revise   Read your report and try to make it better. Combine sentences if you can. Be sure you give the author's name and the book title.

Proofread   Read your report again. Look for mistakes in grammar and spelling. Be sure you use commas, periods, and capital letters correctly.

Share   Make a neat final copy. Share your writing with others.

Crafts/Hobbies

Read pages 274–275 in the **DATABANK**. Find a book about tools that are used in a craft you enjoy. Then write a book report and draw a picture of the craft tools.

Health/Physical Education

Read a book about a famous person in sports. Cut out a sneaker shape from colored paper. Write a book report about the book you read. Copy it on the sneaker shape. Paste your book report onto a larger sheet of paper.

Literature

Find a book of poems by one poet. Write a book report about it. Then tell what two of the poems in the book are about. Give reasons why you liked or did not like the poems.

Mathematics

Read a book about shapes. Write a book report about it. Find pictures that show the shapes of everyday things. Paste the pictures on colored paper.

Science

Find a book that tells how a machine is made or how it works. Write a book report about the book. Then draw a picture to help show how the machine is made or how it works.

Music/Art

Read a book about music or drawing. Write a book report about it. On another sheet of paper, draw or paste pictures of things that are described in the book.

Descriptive Words

STUDY

Some words tell about nouns. These words describe people, places, or things.

Read these sentences. Notice the words in color.

1. Children saw pretty flowers.
2. The happy children laughed.

What word describes the flowers? What word describes the children? The words *pretty* and *happy* are **describing words.** Words that describe nouns are called **adjectives.**

Read these sentences.

3. The bird flew.
4. The tiny bird flew.

What adjective was added in sentence 4? What noun does *tiny* describe? The word *tiny* helps you to picture how the bird looks. Adjectives tell more about nouns.

Read these sentences. As you read, ask yourself these questions. What does the tree look like? What kind of song did the bird sing?

5. The bird sat in a tall tree.
6. The bird sang a loud song.

220

Adjectives are words that describe nouns.

REMEMBER

Finding Adjectives Copy these sentences. Look at the underlined nouns. Draw two lines under the adjective that describes each noun.

PRACTICE

1. Tiny <u>trees</u> grow here.
2. The pond has cool <u>water</u>.
3. The beautiful <u>flowers</u> bloomed.
4. Children play with old <u>dolls</u>.
5. Women wear silk <u>robes</u>.
6. Farmers need large <u>hats</u>.
7. Plants grow in long <u>rows</u>.
8. People make hot <u>drinks</u>.
9. The sweet <u>cherries</u> have pits.
10. Do you like brown <u>rice</u>?

Writing Adjectives Copy and complete each sentence. Use each adjective only once.

soft	sad	new	happy	last

The ___play was good. We heard ___music. A man wore a ___mask. We laughed at the ___ faces. Everyone liked the ___dance.

Sentences Write four sentences about a place you like, such as a park. Use an adjective in each sentence.

WRITE

Words that Tell *How Many* and *What Kind*

You know that adjectives are words that describe nouns. Read these sentences. Notice the words in color.

1. Two fishermen carried the net.

2. They caught several fish.

How many fishermen carried the net? How many fish did they catch? *Two* and *several* are adjectives. They tell *how many.*

Now read these sentences.

3. The small boat rocked up and down.

4. Cold water washed over the boat.

What kind of boat was it? What kind of water washed over the boat? *Small* and *cold* are adjectives. They tell *what kind.*

Now read these sentences. As you read, ask yourself these questions. How many boats set out? What kind of nets did they carry?

5. Ten boats set out.

6. They carried large nets.

☑ Some adjectives tell *how many.*
☑ Some adjectives tell *what kind.*

Finding Adjectives and Nouns   Copy these sentences. Underline each adjective. Circle the noun it describes.

1. Many people went to market.
2. A family walked ten miles.
3. Women sold ripe fruit.
4. They called in loud voices.
5. People talked to old friends.
6. Two people played drums.
7. We looked at a large map.
8. It showed five nations.
9. The busy market closed early.
10. We bought three pretty bowls.

Identifying Adjectives Copy these sentences. Underline each adjective. Write *how many* if the adjective tells how many. Write *what kind* if the adjective tells what kind.

11. Wild animals live here.
12. The lion gives a loud roar.
13. We saw four cubs.
14. Two little cubs played.

A Paragraph Write a paragraph about wild animals. Use adjectives in three sentences. Read pages 288–289 of the **DATABANK**.

Comparative and Superlative Forms

You can use adjectives to compare people, places, or things. Read these sentences. Notice the words in color.

    1. The dog is older than the goat.

    2. The elephant is the oldest of all.

What adjective compares two animals in sentence 1? What ending was added to *old* to form *older*? The ending *-er* is added to the adjective to compare two things.

What adjective compares more than two animals in sentence 2? What ending was added to *old* to form *oldest*? The ending *-est* is added to the adjective to compare more than two things.

Now read these sentences. As you read, ask yourself these questions. Which adjective compares two snakes? Which adjective compares more than two snakes?

    3. This snake is longer than that one.

    4. This is the longest snake of all.

☑ Adjectives can be used to compare nouns.

☑ Add *-er* to most adjectives to compare two nouns.

☑ Add *-est* to most adjectives to compare more than two nouns.

Writing Adjectives Copy and complete the chart. Write the correct form of each adjective.

adjective	*-er* form	*-est* form
1. low	lower	lowest
2. soft		
3. old		
4. hard		
5. clean		

Using Adjectives Copy and complete each sentence. Add *-er* or *-est* to the adjective in ( ).

1. The dress is ___ than the shirt. (long)
2. Sandals are ___ than shoes. (cool)
3. This is the ___ dress of all. (bright)
4. This coat is ___ than that one. (warm)
5. This is the ___ coat I have. (warm)
6. This shirt is ___ than the dress. (new)
7. Cotton is ___ than wool. (light)
8. Which cap is the ___ of all? (small)
☆ 9. People wore their ___ clothing. (light)
☆ 10. Mrs. Rava tells us that cotton is the ___cloth of all. (cool)

A Letter Pretend that you went to a fair. Write a letter to a friend. Tell about three things you saw. Compare them. Use the *-er* and *-est* forms of some adjectives.

Using *A* and *An* Correctly

Two words that come before nouns are *a* and *an*. Read these sentences. Notice the words in color.

1. Maria has a pear.
2. Pedro bites an apple.

What word comes before the noun *pear*? What word comes before the noun *apple*? The word *a* comes before the noun *pear*. The word *an* comes before the noun *apple*.

Read these sentences.

3. Here is a peach.
4. Do you want an orange?

Notice that *a* is used before a noun that begins with a **consonant** sound. *An* is used before a noun that begins with a **vowel** sound.

Read these sentences. As you read, ask yourself these questions. What word comes before each noun? How does each noun begin?

5. We are going to a party.
6. Remember to take an umbrella.

☑ Use *a* before a noun that begins with a **consonant** sound.

☑ Use *an* before a noun that begins with a **vowel** sound.

226

Choosing *A* or *An*   Copy and complete these sentences. Choose the correct word in (   ).

1. The children sang (a, an) song.
2. They did (a, an) dance.
3. The woman wore (a, an) hat.
4. She told us (a, an) story.
5. It was about (a, an) artist.
6. We tapped on (a, an) animal.
7. The boy caught (a, an) fish.
8. Everyone had (a, an) good time.
9. Is that (a, an) alligator?
10. (A, An) bear and (a, an) elephant fell from the animal.

Using *A* or *An*   Copy each sentence. Complete each sentence with *a* or *an*.

11. The town had ___ feast.
12. Visitors came in ___ boat.
13. They stood under ___ umbrella.
14. The girl wore ___ flower.
15. ___child carried ___ animal.

A Funny Story   Write a funny story about something that happened to you when you visited a new place. Draw one line under *a* and two lines under *an* in your sentences.

Capitalization of Proper Adjectives

Some nouns name special people, places, and things. Adjectives can be formed from special nouns. Read these sentences. Notice the words in color.

1. This dish comes from Greece.
2. Try some Greek meatballs.

What special place is named in sentence 1? *Greece* is a noun that names a special place. What special adjective describes meatballs in sentence 2? *Greek* is an adjective. It is formed from the noun *Greece.* Notice that the noun *Greece* begins with a capital letter. The adjective *Greek* also begins with a capital letter.

Now read these sentences. As you read, ask yourself these questions. What noun names a special place? What special adjective describes the noun *cheese*?

3. This cheese comes from Hungary.
4. We like Hungarian cheese.

☑ A **special adjective** can be formed from a special noun.

☑ Begin a special adjective with a capital letter.

228

Finding Special Adjectives

PRACTICE

Copy the menu. Draw a line under each special adjective that comes from the name of a country.

Menu

1. Spanish rice
2. Mexican dip
3. Swedish pancakes
4. Egyptian beans
⭐ 5. North African lemon salad

Capitalizing Special Adjectives

Copy these sentences. Begin each special adjective with a capital letter.

6. They eat dutch noodles.
7. Enjoy this polish soup.
8. Taste the italian salad.
9. Do you like french bread?
10. Try this swiss cheese.
11. This is german meat.
12. They serve a chinese drink.
13. This indian dish has chicken.
14. Rice cakes are a japanese treat.
⭐ 15. Will you taste the south american stew?

A Menu   Write a menu of your own. List three foods that have special names.

WRITE

Introduction to Adverbs

Some words tell more about verbs. These words tell how, when, or where an action takes place.

Read these sentences. Notice the words in color.

1. The people sat outside.

2. They waited quietly.

What word tells where the people sat? What word tells how the people waited? The words *outside* and *quietly* are **adverbs.**

Read these sentences.

3. A man spoke.

4. He spoke loudly.

What adverb was added in sentence 4? What verb does *loudly* tell about? Notice that the adverb in sentence 4 helps you to picture how the man spoke. Adverbs tell more about actions.

Read these sentences. Ask yourself these questions. How did the children wait? How did they watch?

5. The children waited calmly.

6. They watched closely.

☑ An **adverb** tells more about a verb.

☑ An adverb can tell *how, when,* or *where.*

230

Finding Adverbs   Copy these sentences. Circle the adverb that tells about the underlined verb.

1. The fair <u>ends</u> today.
2. Many people <u>arrived</u> early.
3. The red car <u>turned</u> here.
4. They <u>walk</u> quickly.
5. The children <u>laughed</u> happily.
6. Riverboats <u>sailed</u> slowly.
7. The ship <u>docked</u> today.
8. Planes <u>zoomed</u> loudly.
9. Balloons <u>floated</u> upward.
10. Everyone <u>celebrated</u> joyfully.

Writing Adverbs   Copy and complete each sentence. Use each adverb from the box only once.

softly	quietly	inside	now	happily

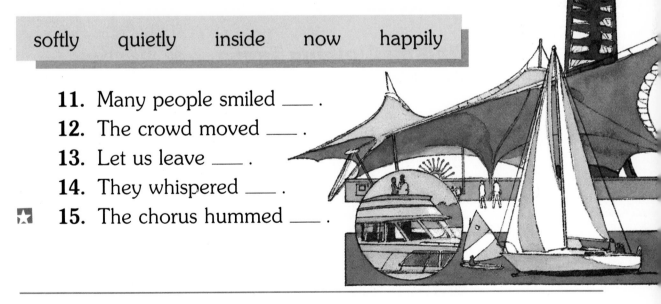

11. Many people smiled ____ .
12. The crowd moved ____ .
13. Let us leave ____ .
14. They whispered ____ .
15. The chorus hummed ____ .

Sentences   Write five sentences about a Fair of All Nations. Use an adverb in each sentence.

Words From Other Languages

STUDY

Many items of clothing have names that come from other countries. The word *pajamas* comes from India. The word *poncho* comes from South America. Here are some other examples.

Item of Clothing	Country	Name
a soft, flat cap	France	beret
leather shorts	Germany	lederhosen
a hooded jacket	Russia	parka
a loose shirt	West Africa	dashiki
a hat with a wide brim	Spain	sombrero
a long, loose robe	Japan	kimono

PRACTICE

Finding Clothing Terms   Use the chart above to find the name of each of the following. Write each name on a piece of paper.

1.   2.   3.

4.   ★ 5.   ★ 6.

WRITE

Writing Sentences   Write a sentence about each item of clothing above. In each sentence, tell how or when you would wear the clothing.

Language and Logic

Drawing Conclusions

Read sentence 1. It is a true sentence.

   1. All cities have buildings.

Now read sentence 2.

   2. Some cities have buildings.

You know that sentence 1 is true. So you can be sure that sentence 2 is also true. That is a **conclusion** you can draw from sentence 1.

If you know a sentence is true, you can draw conclusions from it.

Drawing Conclusions   Copy these

sentences. Suppose each sentence is true. Write a conclusion you can draw from it. Begin each conclusion with *some.*

   1. All countries have citizens.
   2. All countries have governments.
   3. All people have parents.
★ **4.** Plants need water.

Writing Conclusions   Suppose each of these

sentences is true. Copy the sentences. Write one conclusion you can draw from each sentence.

   5. All books have pages.
★ **6.** Many books are long.

Reading a Schedule

Mrs. Green's math class shares a computer with Mr. Lee's math class. This **schedule** shows the times when Mrs. Green's students will use the computer.

COMPUTER SCHEDULE FOR MONDAY

NAMES	TIME
Laura and James	9:00
Marian and Paul	9:30
Bob and Carlos	10:00
Beth and Kim	10:30
Rico and Jan	11:00

What is the title of this schedule? To read the schedule, the students look first for their names. Then they look to the right of their names to find the time they will use the computer.

◢ A **schedule** is a list that tells when certain things will happen.

234

Reading a Schedule   Read the schedule on page 234. Write the answer to each question.

1. How many students will use the computer on Monday?

2. How many students work at one time?

3. When will the first students begin?

4. How many pairs of students will use the computer?

5. Will each pair work for an hour or a half hour?

Using a Schedule   Read the schedule on page 234. Write *Yes* if the sentence is true. Write *No* if it is not true.

6. Marian and Paul will use the computer at 10:00.

7. Rico and Jan will be the last to use the computer.

8. Beth and Kim will work before Bob and Carlos.

9. Laura and James will finish at 9:00.

10. Another pair of students could start working at 11:30.

A Schedule   Write a schedule telling what you would like to do after school today. Tell what you would like to do and the time you would like to do it.

Reading a Graph

Mrs. Green's math class drew a **bar graph.** A graph is a good way to show and compare facts. This graph showed how many students had birthdays in the first half of the year. Look at the graph.

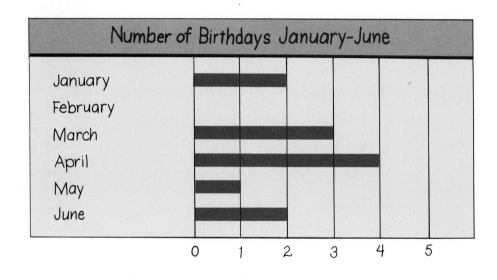

What is the title of the graph? How many months are shown on the graph?

To read this graph, put your finger on one of the bars. Move your finger to the end of the bar. Look at the number below. How many birthdays were there in June?

- ◤ A **graph** can help you understand facts.
- ◤ A graph shows how one fact compares to another.

236

Reading a Graph Look at the graph on page
236. Write answers to these questions.

1. Which month has the most birthdays?
2. Which month has no birthdays at all?
3. Which months have the same number of birthdays?
4. Does May or June have more birthdays?

Using a Graph Look at the graph below and answer the questions.

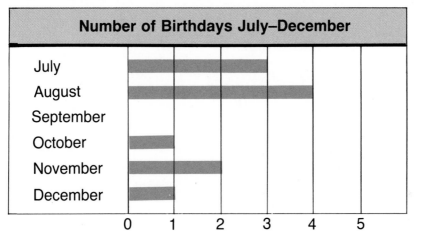

5. How many birthdays are in August?
6. How many birthdays are in July?
7. How many more birthdays are in August than in July?
8. How many birthdays are there in all in October, November, and December?

Sentences Read the information about trees
on page 293 of the **DATABANK**. Look at the graph.
Write five sentences using the facts given in the
graph. Tell about a different tree in each sentence.

Reading a Flowchart

Mrs. Green put this **flowchart** on the chalkboard. It shows the children how to start a computer.

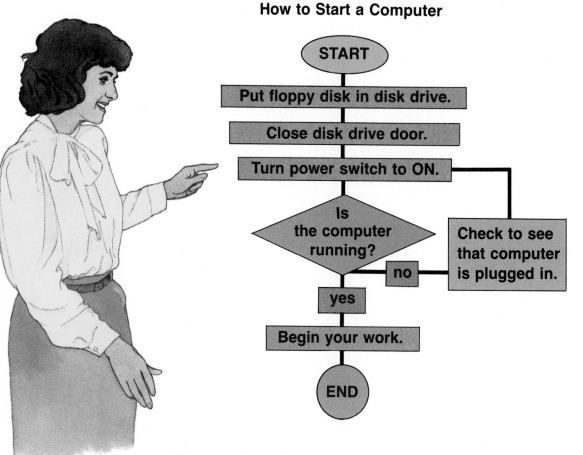

How to Start a Computer

START

Put floppy disk in disk drive.

Close disk drive door.

Turn power switch to ON.

Is the computer running?

Check to see that computer is plugged in.

no

yes

Begin your work.

END

To use this flowchart, the children start at the top circle. They follow the directions in the boxes. When they come to the diamond, they read and answer the question. Then they follow their answers to find out what to do next.

What do you do after you close the disk drive door? What is the question in the diamond?

238

A **flowchart** is a special chart that shows you how to do something.

Completing a Flowchart Copy this flowchart. Write the steps where they belong.

   1. Be sure the calculator is on.
   2. Press the second number to be added.
   3. Read the sum of the two numbers.
   4. Press the button with the equal sign.

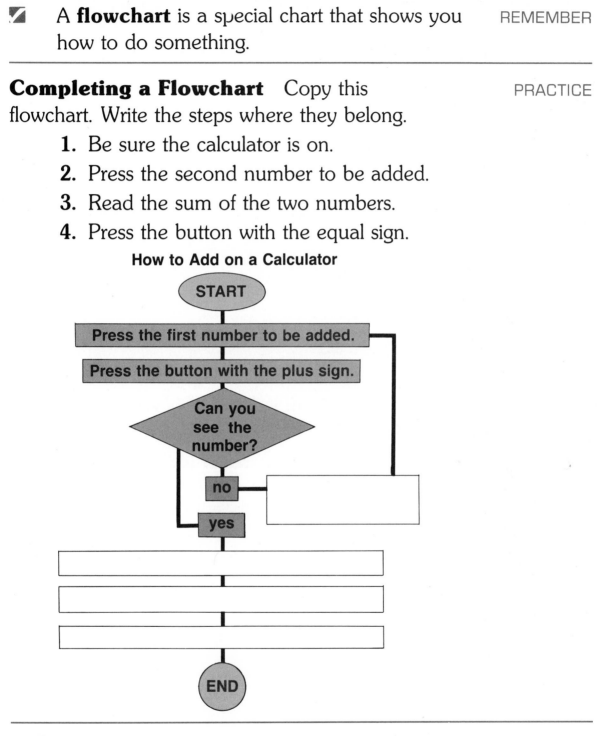

How to Add on a Calculator

START

Press the first number to be added.

Press the button with the plus sign.

Can you see the number?

no

yes

END

A Flowchart Make a flowchart of your own. In the flowchart, show the steps you would take to sharpen a pencil.

Composition   Write a book report about a book that you have read. The book may be fiction or nonfiction.

Grammar, Mechanics, and Usage   Choose the titles that are written correctly.

1. (a) <u>Nate the great</u>   (b) Nate the great
   (c) Nate the Great   (d) <u>Nate the Great</u>

2. (a) to Find a Dinosaur   (b) <u>To Find a Dinosaur</u>
   (c) To Find a dinosaur   (d) To Find a Dinosaur

3. (a) <u>The Wild Colt</u>   (b) The Wild Colt
   (c) <u>the Wild Colt</u>   (d) The wild colt

Choose whether each underlined adjective tells *how many* or *what kind*.

4. John has <u>five</u> books.
   (a) how many
   (b) what kind

5. The water is <u>hot</u>.
   (a) how many
   (b) what kind

6. Here is <u>one</u> penny.
   (a) how many
   (b) what kind

7. I'd like a <u>cool</u> drink.
   (a) how many
   (b) what kind

Choose the correct word to complete each sentence.

8. I am ___ than Sue.
   (a) short   (b) shorter
   (c) shortest

9. I am the ___ of all.
   (a) short   (b) shorter
   (c) shortest

10. Pal is a ___ dog.
    (a) small   (b) smaller
    (c) smallest

11. Pal is ___ than the cat.
    (a) small   (b) smaller
    (c) smallest

Choose <u>a</u> or <u>an</u> to complete each sentence.

12. I ate ___ egg.

    ⓐ a   ⓑ an

13. ___ nice boy helped me.

    ⓐ A   ⓑ An

14. Where is ___ dish?

    ⓐ a   ⓑ an

15. Josh picked ___ apple.

    ⓐ a   ⓑ an

Choose the best way to write each sentence.

16. ⓐ I have a Greek coin.   ⓑ I have a greek coin.

17. ⓐ Dad likes chinese food.   ⓑ Dad likes Chinese food.

18. ⓐ I'll buy Italian bread.   ⓑ I'll buy italian bread.

Choose the adverb in each sentence.

19. He walked slowly home.

    ⓐ   ⓑ   ⓒ   ⓓ

20. My class begins early.

    ⓐ   ⓑ   ⓒ   ⓓ

21. I smiled happily at Dad.

    ⓐ   ⓑ   ⓒ   ⓓ

22. The boat left today.

    ⓐ   ⓑ   ⓒ   ⓓ

Practical Language Skills   Choose the correct word to complete each sentence.

23. A ___ is a list that tells when certain things will take place.

    ⓐ schedule   ⓑ graph   ⓒ flow chart

24. A ___ is a special chart that shows steps in order.

    ⓐ schedule   ⓑ graph   ⓒ flow chart

25. A ___ shows how one fact compares to another.

    ⓐ schedule   ⓑ graph   ⓒ flow chart

Writing Sentences Correctly (pages 10–11, 26–27)

Write each sentence correctly.

1. what a lovely coat
2. will John play
3. he liked the book
4. please sit down

Nouns (pages 54–59)

Copy each group of words. Then ring the nouns.

5. car   talk   boat
6. dancer   school   sang
7. went   boy   rock
8. water   see   library

Adding -s to Action Verbs (pages 90–91)

Copy each sentence. Write each underlined verb correctly.

9. The boy <u>hang</u> up his coat.
10. Our cat <u>eat</u> pickles!
11. That tree <u>grow</u> slowly.

Capitalizing Nouns (pages 60–63, 118–119, 128–129)

Write each noun correctly.

12. memorial day
13. t. r. jones
14. friday
15. mr. sam lee
16. park street
17. february

Writing a Descriptive Paragraph (pages 148–149)

Write a descriptive paragraph about what you see as you look out of your classroom window. Begin with a sentence that tells what the paragraph is about. Remember to add details that describe what you see.

SKILLS

Prefixes and Suffixes   (pages 170–173)

Write the meaning of each word.

18. refill   **19.** unseen   **20.** joyful

Commas   (pages 50–51, 84–85, 152–153, 186–187)

Write each sentence correctly.

21. Today is May 1 1988.

22. I live in Dallas Texas.

23. The girls ran swam and fished.

Pronouns   (pages 190–195)

Use each of the pronouns below in a sentence.

24. you **25.** she **26.** him **27.** them **28.** I

How-To Paragraphs and Book Reports (pages 181–183, 211–213)

Finish each sentence with the words *how-to paragraph* or *book report*

29. A _____ tells how to make or do something.

30. A _____ gives an author and a title.

31. A _____ gives a list of materials needed.

Verbs, Adverbs, and Adjectives   (pages 156–163, 220–223, 230–231)

Copy each sentence. Underline the verb. Ring the adverb. Write X on the adjective.

32. The seven girls ran quickly.

33. The hot sun shines brightly.

34. The three boys are busy today.

CONTENTS

244

CAPITALIZATION

REMEMBER

Names and Initials of People and Pets

☑ Begin names of people, pets, and initials with capital letters.

Muffin   **S**ally **J. B**rown

☑ Begin a person's title with a capital letter.

Ms. Williams   **M**r. Jackson
Dr. Atkins

PRACTICE

A. Write each name and title correctly.

1. ellen h. stokes
2. kippy
3. mrs. gail j. cates
4. mr. bruce jones
5. mittens
6. dr. taku ogara

B. Copy these sentences. Use capital letters where they are needed.

7. On Tuesday judy and jeff came to visit.
8. They brought grandma and grandpa with them.
9. Did you see the present judy brought jamie?
10. It was a kitten named sam.

246

Place Names

✓ Begin each word in the name of a special place with a capital letter.

New York City Santa Barbara Maine
Rocky Mountains   Nile River
Golden Gate Park

✓ Begin a special adjective with a capital letter.

German   Spanish   Greek

A. Write each place name and each special adjective correctly.

1. japanese
2. bay avenue
3. long island sound
4. irish
5. english
6. redwood national park

B. Copy these sentences. Use capital letters where they are needed.

7. Abby, Amos, and Rosa went on a picnic to rock creek park.

8. They ate swiss cheese sandwiches on french bread.

9. They swam in crystal lake.

10. They bought some african daisies and some dutch tulips at a flower stand.

DATABANK · CAPITALIZATION

CAPITALIZATION

Days, Months, and Holidays

☑ Begin days of the week, months of the year, and holidays with capital letters.

Tuesday   November   Thanksgiving

Pronoun *I*

☑ Write the word *I* as a capital letter.

First Words

☑ Begin statements, questions, exclamations, and commands with capital letters.

PRACTICE

Copy these sentences. Use capital letters where they are needed.

1. we are going to Mr. Creeg's house.
2. did Paula have a party on valentine's day?
3. oh no, i lost my new gloves!
4. bring your halloween costume to my house next sunday.
5. what a wonderful party we went to on new year's day!
6. where did i put my glasses?
7. please return the book by next wednesday.
8. is Jenny coming over for dinner on friday?
9. labor day is the first monday in september.
10. my brother and i always go camping on the third saturday in july.

PUNCTUATION
Period, Question Mark, and Exclamation Point

To End Sentences

☑ Use a period to end a statement or a command.

> We like to take long walks.
> Please close the window.

☑ Use a question mark to end a question.

> Where did Sara go**?**

☑ Use an exclamation point to end an exclamation.

> What a wonderful song they sang**!**

Copy these sentences. Use correct punctuation.

1. Oh no, I broke my glasses

2. Please bring me my notebook

3. What time is it

4. What a wonderful book I read

5. Listen to Jared play the piano

6. Why was Carlos late for the meeting

7. Yellow is my favorite color

8. Do you know where Cora put my coat

★ **9.** Tim asked me if I wanted to go to the zoo

★ **10.** You asked Janet for help, didn't you

PUNCTUATION
Comma

In Dates

☑ Use a comma between the day and the year in a date.

> September 6, 1951   April 21, 1990

In Addresses

☑ Use a comma between the names of the city and the state in an address.

> Los Angeles, California   Houston, Texas

A. Write these dates and addresses correctly.

1. June 24 1989
2. April 8 1990
3. Akron Ohio
4. December 14 1991
5. Denver Colorado
6. St. Louis Missouri

B. Copy these sentences. Use correct punctuation.

7. Yvette lives in Honolulu Hawaii.
8. Have you ever been to Nome Alaska?
9. Grace is going to Cape Cod Massachusetts.
☆ 10. Peter visited Washington D.C.

250

Comma

In Letters

REMEMBER

☑ Use a comma after the greeting of a friendly letter.

    Dear Max,   Dear Angela,

☑ Use a comma after the closing of a letter.

    Sincerely yours,   Your friend,

In a Series

☑ Use commas when you list three or more words in a sentence.

    Larry's new kite is orange, blue, and white.

Copy this letter. Use correct punctuation.

PRACTICE

Dear Zachary

    Last Saturday my Aunt Lily took me to the circus. I saw elephants lions tigers and horses. There were many funny clowns. They drove tiny cars walked on stilts and did somersaults. I really had a good time.

            Your friend
            Beth

DATABANK · PUNCTUATION

THESAURUS

Use this thesaurus when you need help in thinking of the word that says exactly what you mean. The entry words are in heavy type and are arranged in alphabetical order. Each entry word is followed by one or more synonyms. Some entries end with one or more words in blue type. These are anyonyms of the entry word.

Some entry words, such as *club,* have more than one meaning. There is a separate entry for each meaning. Each entry is numbered.

A

act   perform, behave

active   lively lazy

afraid   frightened, scared, alarmed unafraid, fearless

answer   reply, response question

arrive   come, reach, get to leave

article   story, essay, report

attach   fasten, join, connect, add detach

awful   terrible, horrible pleasant

B

bad   evil, naughty good

bat   1. club, stick
       2. strike, hit

beach   shore, coast, seaside

beautiful   attractive, lovely, pretty, handsome ugly

big   1. large, huge, tremendous, enormous, immense small

big   2. important, great, grand, considerable unimportant

break   fracture, crack, crush, split, smash, shatter mend, fix

bright   smart, alert, intelligent dull

by   near, beside, at

C

call   1. shout, yell

call   2. telephone

careful   cautious, watchful careless

choose   pick, select, elect,

chop   cut, cleave, sever, hack

clean   spotless, spick-and-span dirty

club   1. group, association

club   2. bat, stick

club   3. strike, hit, knock

cold   chilly, frosty, icy hot

correct   1. right, true, accurate, proper, exact, appropriate incorrect, wrong

correct   2. improve, remedy

cry   weep, wail, sob, bawl

D

dangerous   unsafe, risky safe

dark   dim, gloomy, dreary bright

dirty   soiled, filthy clean

divide   separate, split unite

drag   pull, tug, draw, haul, tow

draw   1. drag, move, pull, tug

draw   2. etch, outline, sketch

drizzle   rain, shower, sprinkle

252

E

earth **1.** soil, dirt, ground

earth **2.** world, globe

easy simple, plain   hard

empty blank, vacant, hollow, barren   full

end finish, stop, complete, quit   begin

energy strength, force, power, might, vitality, pep, vigor

exit depart, go out, leave   enter

express **1.** fast, quick, speedy, rapid, swift   slow

express **2.** present, tell, describe

F

fable story, fairy tale, legend, myth

fact detail, item, point

fair **1.** right, correct, just, honest, impartial   unfair, unjust

fair **2.** sunny, clear, bright   cloudy

fair **3.** light, pale   dark

false **1.** wrong, incorrect, untrue   true

false **2.** fake, counterfeit   real

fast rapid, swift, speedy, quick   slow

fat heavy, stout, plump, chubby   thin, lean

find discover, learn, uncover   lose

flat smooth, even, level   uneven

force **1.** make, drive, push

force **2.** power, strength, energy

friend buddy, pal   enemy

G

garbage trash, waste, junk

gate fence, barrier

gift present, offering

give present, hand over   take

glad happy, pleased, cheerful, delighted, joyful   unhappy

good fine, nice, proper, right, appropriate, decent   bad

great grand, glorious, splendid, wonderful, sensational, fantastic

H

handsome good-looking, attractive   ugly

happy glad, cheerful, joyful, jolly, gay, pleased   unhappy, sad

hard **1.** firm, solid, stiff, rigid   soft

hard **2.** difficult, tough, rough   easy

heavy fat, stout, plump   thin

help aid, cooperate, support, assist

hint clue, suggestion

huge gigantic, colossal, enormous   tiny

I

idea thought, notion, concept

imagine **1.** think, guess, suppose, believe

imagine **2.** dream, fantasize, envision

interesting entertaining, amusing, fascinating   boring, uninteresting

invent make up, develop, create, originate, produce, discover, devise

J

jam **1.** crowd, stuff, cram, squeeze, crush, load

jam **2.** jelly, marmalade, preserve

job work, employment, task, assignment, duty, position

DATABANK · THESAURUS

THESAURUS

join connect, unite, combine, link, attach separate, detach

jump spring, leap, bound

K

key **1.** clue, hint, evidence, lead

key **2.** pitch, tone, note

kind **1.** considerate, thoughtful, gentle, helpful unkind, mean

kind **2.** sort, type, variety

knock hit, strike, beat, bang

L

large big, huge, tremendous, enormous, immense small

laugh giggle, chuckle

leap jump, spring, bound

learn **1.** find out, discover

learn **2.** memorize

leave **1.** go, depart, exit arrive

leave **2.** quit, desert stay

let permit, allow, consent

light **1.** bright, clear dark

light **2.** weightless, airy heavy

little small, tiny, minute big

lock fasten close, hook, clasp, latch, shut unlock, open

look **1.** see, glance, gaze, stare

look **2.** seem, appear

loud noisy, roaring soft

M

mad **1.** crazy, insane sane

mad **2.** angry, furious, enraged, annoyed, cross, irritated

make **1.** build, construct, create, produce, form, assemble

make **2.** force, cause, compel

make **3.** kind, type, sort, brand

match context, game, battle

messy sloppy, careless, untidy, dirty neat

middle center, heart, core, hub

N

name label, title

nap sleep, doze, drowse, snooze

near close, at hand far

need want, lack, require

noise racket, clamor, uproar quiet

normal regular, usual, typical, standard, ordinary unusual

nosy snoopy, curious, prying

now immediately, instantly, at once, promptly, presently later

O

obey listen to, mind, comply disobey

odor smell, scent, aroma, fragrance

only just, simply, merely

open start, begin, launch close

own have, possess

P

pack fill, load, stuff empty

pail bucket

paint **1.** coat, color, cover

paint **2.** picture, draw, illustrate, portray, depict

pal friend, buddy, chum

path route, way, track, trail, lane, road

pick choose, select, elect

pile heap, stack, mound

pleasant pleasing, likable, appealing, agreeable, cheerful, delightful unpleasant

254

plenty   a lot, enough, ample

practice   drill, exercise, train

prepare   get ready, fix, arrange

pretty   attractive, lovely, good-looking   homely, unattractive

protect   defend, shield, cover

pull   tug, tow, draw, drag, yank, haul   push

Q

question   ask, inquire   answer

quiet   silent, still   noisy, loud

quit   stop, end, finish   continue

R

race 1.   run, speed, rush, dash, hurry

race 2.   nationality, ancestry

ready   prepared, set   unprepard

receive   take in, get, gain   give

report   tell, recite, narrate, state, describe, recount

rest   pause, relax, unwind

return 1.   go back, revisit

return 2.   give back, repay

rip   tear, cut, split, slit, slash

run 1.   race, hurry, jog, sprint

run 2.   govern, control, regulate, command, manage, head, lead

run 3.   operate, work

run 4.   flow, stream, pour, gush

S

sad   unhappy, depressed, blue, downcast, gloomy, glum   happy

sag   droop, hang, drag

save 1.   keep, preserve, conserve, store, accumulate   spend, discard

save 2.   rescue, recover, retrieve

say   speak, tell, declare, state, exclaim, express, remark, comment, mention, utter

scratch   cut, mark, scrape, scar

seal 1.   fasten, secure, bind, close, shut   open

seal 2.   stamp, sign, mark

seal 3.   sea lion

seem   appear, look

separate   divide, split, part, sort   join

shake   tremble, shudder, shiver, quiver, vibrate

show 1.   demonstrate, illustrate, indicate, explain, clarify

show 2.   performance, presentation, production, exhibit

shut   close, fasten, lock, seal   open

skinny   thin, lean, slim   chubby

skip   pass over, leave out, miss   include

sleep   doze, nap, snooze, slumber

slide   glide, skid, slip

sloppy   careless, messy, untidy   neat

small   little, slight, puny   big

smile   grin, smirk   frown

soft   quiet   loud

sore   painful, aching, tender

sparkle   shine, flash, glimmer, glitter, glisten, twinkle

special   unusual, exceptional, outstanding, extraordinary, remarkable   ordinary

speedy   fast, rapid, swift, quick,   hasty

spot 1.   soil, dirty, stain, smudge

spot 2.   pick out, recognize, identify, spy, sight, distinguish

THESAURUS

stop end, halt, quit start

storm gale, hurricane, tornado

strength power, force, might, energy, vigor weakness

strike hit, bat, slap, smack, slug, swat, knock

strong mighty, powerful, sturdy, hardy, tough, healthy weak

surprise astonish, astound, amaze, startle, shock, stun

sweet 1. charming, lovely, pleasant, agreeable, adorable disagreeable

sweet 2. sugary

switch change, exchange, swap, trade, substitute

T

tag label, name, brand

take 1. capture, get, obtain give

take 2. carry, bring, transport

taste sample, test, try, savor

teach instruct, show, educate, inform, tell, advise, tutor

terrible horrible, horrid, dreadful, awful, atrocious wonderful

terrific marvelous, wonderful, glorious, great, magnificent, superb, sensational ordinary

thin skinny, lean, slim, slender fat

think 1. believe, suppose, imagine, expect, guess, suspect

think 2. consider, reflect, ponder

train 1. teach, drill, practice, exercise, prepare, condition

train 2. railroad cars

trip 1. stumble, tumble, fall

trip 2. tour, journey, excursion

U

under below, beneath above, over

unhappy sad, depressed, blue, downcast, gloomy, glum happy

useful helpful, practical, handy, valuable, beneficial useless

V

vacation leave, break, recess, holiday

vote ballot, choice, selection

W

wake get up, arise

watch 1. observe, see, look at

watch 2. guard, protect, defend

whole complete, total, entire partial

wish desire, long for, want, crave

wonderful fabulous, marvelous, glorious, great, grand, magnificent, splendid, superb, divine, sensational, spectacular horrible

worried troubled, concerned, disturbed, upset, nervous calm

wreck destroy, ruin, demolish

wrong incorrect, inaccurate, faulty, mistaken right

X

x ray picture, photograph

Y

yank pull, tug, jerk

yarn wool, thread

yell shout, scream, howl, cry, call, shriek, screech

Z

zero nothing, nil, none

zoom speed, zip, whiz, fly

256

SPELLING LIST

A

across
add
afternoon
age
air
and
ant
any
apple
are
aren't
arm
art
as
ask
ate
aunt
away

B

baby
back
bad
bag
ball
baseball

bat
become
bee
been
before
beg
begin
being
bell
below
bend
big
bike
bikes
bird
birthday
bit
blew
blue
book
born
both
bottom
box
boxes
boy
boys
bread
brother
bug

bump
burn
buses
but
buy
by

C

cake
call
came
can
cannot
can't
car
cat
chair
children
circle
circus
clap
class
classes
clay
clean
climb
clock
club

come
cook
cookie
corn
could
couldn't
cross
cry
cup
cupcake
cut

D

dad
day
dear
desk
did
didn't
dig
dime
dirt
dishes
does
dog
doll
don't
door
dot

SPELLING LIST

dress
drink
drop
dug

E
each
eat
eating
egg
eight
end
evening
eye

F
fair
fall
farm
fast
father
fed
fern
find
first
fit
five

flag
floor
fly
food
foot
football
for
fork
four
fox
foxes
free
friend
frog
full
fun
fur

G
game
games
garden
gate
get
gift
girl
give
glad
glass

glow
going
gone
good
good-by
grade
great
green
grow
guess
guesses

H
had
hair
half
hammer
handle
happens
happier
happy
hard
has
hasn't
hate
have
haven't
head
helped

helping
here
here's
hid
high
him
his
home
hop
hope
horn
horse
hot
hour
houses
how
huff
hug
hundred
hunger
hungry
hurt

I
if
inside
into
is
it's

258

J

jar
jet
job
jump
just

K

keep
kick
kid
kind
king
kiss
know

L

leaf
led
leg
let
light
like
line
lock
look
looking

lot
love
low

M

mad
made
make
making
man
map
mask
may
maybe
men
met
middle
mile
milk
mind
mine
minute
miss
mom
money
moon
mop
more
morning

most
mother
mud
must
my
myself

N

name
nap
net
new
night
no
not
now
nurse
nut

O

off
old
once
one
only
or
orange
other

outside
over
own
ox

P

page
paint
pair
pancake
part
party
pass
pay
pen
penny
pet
pick
picnic
pig
place
plan
planted
planting
plants
play
played
playing

SPELLING LIST

please

pop

pot

puff

pull

purr

purse

put

R

rabbit

race

rain

raincoat

read

reading

red

report

riding

right

road

rock

rode

room

rope

round

rug

run

S

said

same

sat

say

school

see

seem

sell

send

sent

set

seven

shall

she

shell

ship

shirt

shoe

shop

short

should

shouldn't

show

shut

sick

side

sip

sit

six

skirt

sleep

small

smile

some

something

sometime

soon

spell

spin

sport

spot

spring

square

stair

stand

star

stay

stayed

staying

step

stick

still

stir

stood

stop

stopped

store

story

summer

sun

swam

swell

swim

T

table

tag

take

talked

talking

tall

teacher

tell

ten

than

that's

their

them

then

there

there's

these

they

those

three

threw

time

to

260

told
too
toys
train
tree
trees
trip
trips
try
tub
tug
turn
two

U
under
up
upon

V
very
vote

W
walk
walking
wall
was
wasn't
water
way
week
weekend
well
went
were
wet

what
when
where
where's
which
while
white
who
why
will
win
window
winter
wishes
woman
women
won
won't

work
working
would
wouldn't
write
writing

Y
yellow
yes
you
your
yours

Z
zero
zoo

DATABANK · SPELLING LIST

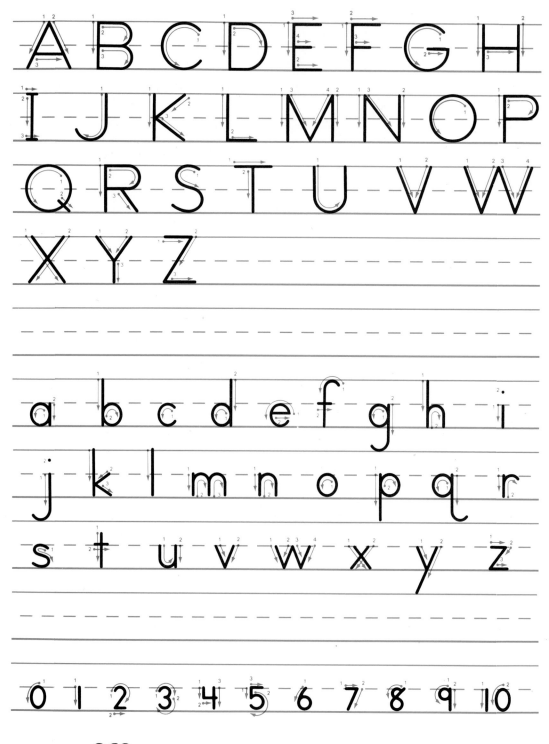

A B C D E F

G H I J K L

M N O P Q R S

T U V W X Y Z

a b c d e f

g h i j k l

m n o p q r s

t u v w x y z

0 1 2 3 4 5 6 7 8 9 10

Headlines
by Malcolm Hall

The animals were putting the newspaper to bed. "Putting a paper to bed" doesn't mean tucking it in for the night, of course. It means getting ready to print the paper.

They all worked together. Frank Beaver read each story aloud. Caroline Porcupine took tiny metal letters, called type, out of a wooden box. These letters spelled out the stories.

Then the Jeremy P. Rat family carried the type, one letter at a time, over to the printing press. Morris Squirrel put the letters on a wide tray. There the type would be used to print the paper.

Theodore Cat was the editor of the paper. It was his job to read the stories and decide which ones to print. Most of the time, however, Theodore just sat at his desk thinking about what a great editor he was.

Oscar Raccoon, a reporter, walked up to Theodore. Oscar was mad! He had written a story, but Theodore wouldn't put it in the paper.

"Why won't you print my story?" asked Oscar. Theodore put his paws over his eyes.

The truth was that Theodore hadn't even read Oscar's story. But Theodore did not want to admit it. So he made up a reason.

"Your story was too long, Oscar."

"But my story was only half a page long," said Oscar.

"Then it was too short," said Theodore. And Theodore leaned back in his chair and smiled as only a cat can.

Theodore trotted over to the printing press. Wheels were turning; ink was splashing; paper was spinning around. Hundreds of tiny letters were printing the news. Suddenly the printing press shot out the first copy of the newspaper. Wham! Right into Theodore's stomach.

Theodore got up slowly and dusted himself off. Then he picked up the paper and started to read. Then Theodore's face fell. He began to pull his fur. When he found his fur was too short, he pulled his whiskers instead.

"Stop the presses," yowled Theodore. Everything came to a stop. Frank began to bite at his nails. Caroline started to knit. The Jeremy P. Rat family ran underneath the printing press and peeped out nervously.

Theodore held up the paper. "Who wrote this headline?" he shouted.

Everyone stared. The headline said: SaDeeRoBanks.

"Can anyone read it?"

For a moment no one spoke. Then Humphrey Snake began to clear his throat. This took quite a while because Humphrey had quite a long throat.

Finally, Humphrey was able to speak. "It says, SaDe eRoB anks!"

All of the animals gasped. Some even began to clap their hands.

Theodore said, "Very good, Humphrey, but what does it mean?"

Suddenly Oscar spoke up. "I can read it," he said, "and I know what it means, too. The headline says, **Sad Deer Rob Banks**."

Oscar had figured out how to read the headline. The last letter of one word was also the first letter of the next word.

"Who did this to my story?" cried Theodore. "This afternoon six deer robbed five banks. After a while, they felt so sorry for the animals whose money they had taken, they began to cry. So my headline was **Sad Deer Rob Banks**. We have to fix it!"

But there was nothing the animals could do about the headline. It was too late to print the paper over again. So the next day, when the paper came out, the headline still said: **SaDeeRoBanks.**

At first, the animals who bought the paper were puzzled. Then they learned how to read the headlines. "Very clever," they said to one another.

When night came, the animals were ready once more to put their paper to bed. And once more Theodore and Oscar were arguing.

"You still haven't put my story in the paper," said Oscar, "and I want to know why not."

"I'm worried about more important things, Oscar," said Theodore. "We've got to make sure that never happens again."

"But, Theodore," said Oscar, "that's what my story is all about! You see, the rats in our office aren't ordinary rats, they're—"

But Theodore wasn't listening.

"I can't talk to you now, Oscar," said Theodore. "As you can see, I'm a very busy man....I mean I'm a very busy cat. No, that's not right either," cried Theodore. "I'm a very busy body!" And Theodore slammed his paw down on his desk so hard all of his telephones began to ring at once.

As the days went by, the headlines kept coming out wrong. One day the paper said: **NoblElKisSecretly.**

That story was about a king and queen elk who were in love. Another day there was a story about a family of geese who went to live in the forest. This time the headline said: **GigglinGeesEnjoYelloWillows.**

The readers of the newspaper liked figuring out the headlines. It gave them something to do while they were riding the bus. But Theodore didn't know this. All day long, he paced up and down the newspaper office, crying, "Woe! Woe!"

No matter how hard Oscar tried to talk to Theodore, Theodore wouldn't listen. Finally, Oscar lost his temper. He tackled Theodore and sat on his chest.

"Theodore," said Oscar, "you've got to listen to me. My story is about the mystery of the headlines."

Theodore blinked his eyes. "Why didn't you tell me this before?" demanded Theodore.

Oscar led Theodore over to the printing press. "Look underneath the printing press, Theodore," said Oscar.

Theodore bent over and looked underneath. There he saw a small house made from tiny metal letters. And inside the house was the Jeremy P. Rat family.

"So it was you rats all along," said Theodore, "stealing letters. Well, I'll fix you!"

"Please, Theodore," said Jeremy, "we didn't mean any harm. We only took the letters you used twice in a row. Besides, we couldn't help it. You see, we're not *ordinary* rats. We're *pack* rats. That's what the *P* in my name stands for," Jeremy said proudly.

"That doesn't matter," said Theodore, and he started to sharpen his claws.

But just then Frank came in with a big pile of mail. "Theodore," said Frank, "look at all the letters. They're from our readers. Everybody likes our headlines."

Theodore was astonished. He coughed and pulled at one ear. Then he said, "Of course they like our headlines. They were my idea all along."

All of the animals looked at one another and groaned. But no one said anything because they knew Theodore would never learn. So Theodore agreed to let the pack rats live in their house beneath the printing press. And he also agreed to print Oscar's story at last. The headline said:
EAGERATSTEALETTERS.

How to Use a Tape Recorder

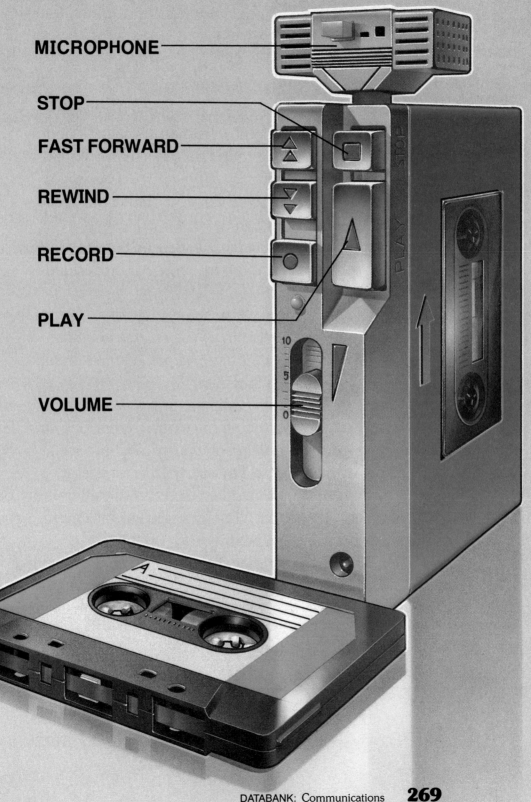

MICROPHONE

STOP

FAST FORWARD

REWIND

RECORD

PLAY

VOLUME

10
5
0

PLAY

STOP

The Goat in the Rug

As told to Charles L. Blood and Martin Link by Geraldine

This is the true story of a weaver and her goat who lived in the Navajo Nation at Window Rock, Arizona.

My name is Geraldine and I live near a place called Window Rock with my Navajo friend, Glenmae. It's called Window Rock because it has a big round hole in it that looks like a window open to the sky.

Glenmae is called Glenmae most of the time because it's easier to say than her Indian name: Glee 'Nasbah. In English that means something like female warrior, but she's really a Navajo weaver. I guess that's why, one day, she decided to weave me into a rug.

I remember it was a warm sunny afternoon. Glenmae had spent most of the morning sharpening a large pair of scissors. I had no idea what she was going to use them for, but it didn't take me long to find out.

Before I knew what was happening, I was on the ground and Glenmae was clipping off my wool in great long strands. (It's called mohair, really.) It didn't hurt at all, but I admit I kicked up my heels some. I'm very ticklish for a goat.

I might have looked a little naked and silly afterwards, but my, did I feel nice and cool! So I decided to stick around and see what would happen next.

The first thing Glenmae did was chop up roots from a yucca plant. The roots made a soapy, rich lather when she mixed them with water. She washed my wool in the suds until it was clean and white.

After that, a little bit of me (you might say) was hung up in the sun to dry. When my wool was dry, Glenmae took out two large square combs with many teeth.

By combing my wool between these carding combs, as they're called, she removed any bits of twigs or burrs and straightened out the fibers. She told me it helped make a smoother yarn for spinning.

Then, Glenmae carefully started to spin my wool—one small bundle at a time—into yarn. I was beginning to find out it takes a long while to make a Navajo rug.

Again and again, Glenmae twisted and pulled, twisted and pulled the wool. Then she spun it around a long, thin stick she called a spindle. As she twisted and pulled and spun, the finer, stronger, and smoother the yarn became.

A few days later, Glenmae and I went for a walk. She said we were going to find some special plants she would use to make dye.

I didn't know what "dye" meant, but it sounded like a picnic to me. I do love to eat plants. That's what got me into trouble.

While Glenmae was out looking for more plants, I ate every one she had already collected in her bucket. Delicious!

The next day, Glenmae made me stay home while she walked miles to a store. She said the dye she could buy wasn't the same as the kind she makes from plants, but since I'd made such a pig of myself, it would have to do.

I was really worried that she would still be angry with me when she got back. She wasn't, though, and pretty soon she had three big potfuls of dye boiling over a fire.

Then I saw what Glenmae had meant by dyeing. She dipped my white wool into one pot…and it turned pink! She dipped it in again. It turned a darker pink! By the time she'd finished dipping it in and out and hung it up to dry, it was a beautiful deep red.

After that, she dyed some of my wool brown, and some of it black. I couldn't help wondering if those plants I'd eaten would turn all of me the same colors.

While I was worrying about that, Glenmae started to make our rug. She took a ball of yarn and wrapped it around and around two poles. I lost count when she'd reached three hundred wraps. I guess I was too busy thinking about what it would be like to be the only red, white, black and brown goat at Window Rock.

It wasn't long before Glenmae had finished wrapping. Then she hung the poles with the yarn on a big wooden frame. It looked like a picture frame made of logs—she called it a "loom."

After a whole week of getting ready to weave, Glenmae started. She began weaving at the bottom of the loom. Then, one strand of yarn at a time, our rug started growing toward the top.

A few strands of black. A few of brown. A few of red. In and out. Back and forth. Until, in a few days, the pattern of our rug was clear to see.

Our rug grew very slowly. Just as every Navajo weaver before her had done for hundreds and hundreds of years, Glenmae formed a design that would never be duplicated.

Then, at last, the weaving was finished! But not until I'd checked it quite thoroughly in front...and in back, did I let Glenmae take our rug off the loom.

There was a lot of me in that rug. I wanted it to be perfect. And it was.

Since then, my wool has grown almost long enough for Glenmae and me to make another rug. I hope we do very soon. Because, you see, there aren't too many weavers like Glenmae left among the Navajos.

And there's only one goat like me, Geraldine.

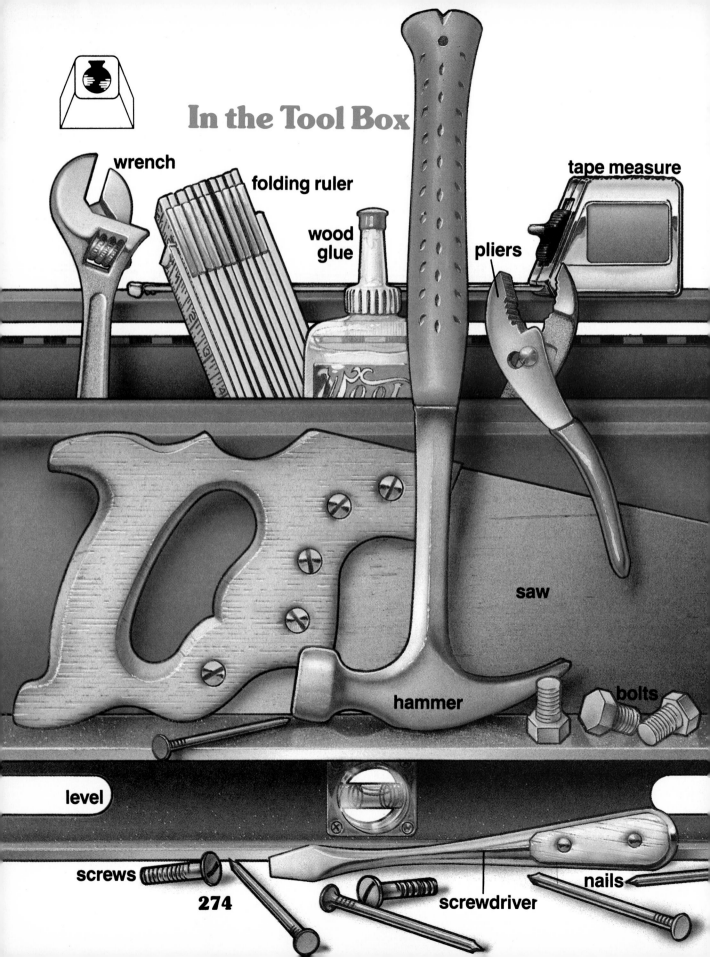

In the Tool Box

wrench

folding ruler

wood glue

tape measure

pliers

saw

hammer

bolts

level

screws

274

screwdriver

nails

A Crafts Fair

The children at Summer Valley School are having a crafts fair. Here are some things that they made.

These things were made of clay.

The pig was made of papier-mâché.

These things were made from several pieces of wood.

The Four Basic Food Groups

Most foods belong to one of four basic food groups. These groups are the **meat group,** the **bread and cereal group,** the **fruit and vegetable group,** and the **milk group.** It is important to eat foods from all four food groups each day.

Here is a list of some of the foods that belong to each group.

Meat Group	Milk Group	Bread and Cereal Group	Fruit and Vegetable Group	
Beef	Milk	Biscuits	Apples	Tomatoes
Chicken	Cheese	Crackers	Bananas	Oranges
Beans, Nuts	Cream	Breads	Grapes	Grapefruit
Eggs	Yogurt	Cereals	Peaches	Broccoli
Fish		Pasta	Plums	Carrots
Peanut Butter			Potatoes	Peas
Pork				Squash
				Mango

At the Football Game

Football is a game for two teams. When your team carries or throws the ball over the goal line, it is called a *touchdown*. A touchdown is worth six points. If a player can kick the football between the *goalposts*, the team scores an extra point. While watching the game, you can eat a bag of *peanuts* or some *popcorn*.

Picnic Games

The spring picnic had started. Some of the children decided to play "Duck, Duck, Goose." They all sat in a wide circle, and they chose Mina to be the goose. Mina walked around the outside of the circle and tapped each child on the head. With each tap, Mina said, "Duck." When Mina tapped Todd on the head, she said, "Goose!" Todd jumped and chased Mina around the circle. Mina got back to Todd's space first and sat down. Then Todd was the goose.

Todd walked around the circle, tapping the children on the head. He decided to walk around two times. When Todd tapped Shawn on the head, he said, "Goose!" As they were running, Shawn tagged Todd before they reached Shawn's place. Todd was goose again.

The children played until everyone had a chance to be goose. It was a great way to have fun.

The Magic Porridge Pot
by Paul Galdone

Once upon a time, long, long ago, a little girl and her mother lived in a small cottage at the end of the village street. They were so poor that often there was nothing to eat in the house but a small piece of bread.

When their cupboard was bare, the little girl would go into the forest near the cottage to search for nuts and berries. One chilly morning she wandered through the dark forest, but she could not find a single nut or berry. At last the little girl sat down on a fallen tree and started to cry.

"There's no food for Mother and me. What will we do? We're so hungry."

"Cheer up, my dear," said a pleasant but crackly voice.

The little girl looked up in surprise to see an old woman who wore a long cloak and leaned on a crooked stick.

"Do not worry, my dear," said the old woman. "You need never be hungry again."

From under her cloak she drew out a small black pot.

"This is a magic pot, my dear. After you put it on the fire, you must say to it, 'Boil, Little Pot, boil!' and at once it will fill up with delicious porridge. When you have had all you can eat, you must say to it, 'Stop, Little Pot, stop!' and the magic pot will stop boiling."

"Oh, thank you so much," said the little girl.

"Never forget the magic words, my dear," said the old woman. "Never forget!"

And no sooner had she said this than she vanished.

The little girl carried the pot home as fast as she could run through the forest.

"What have you there?" her mother asked.

"This is a magic pot that will cook delicious porridge," the little girl explained. "An old woman gave it to me in the forest."

The little girl was eager to try out the magic pot. She set it on the fire and said, "Boil, Little Pot, boil!" Sure enough, delicious porridge bubbled up. When they had had all that they could eat, the little girl said, "Stop, Little Pot, stop!" and the magic pot stopped boiling.

For a long time the little girl and her mother had as much porridge as they wanted, and were very happy and contented.

Then one day the little girl decided to visit her friend at the other end of the village. The little girl was gone a long while and her mother began to be hungry. So she set the magic pot on the fire and said to it, "Boil, Little Pot, boil!" The porridge began to rise in the pot, and the mother dished out a nice bowlful.

Soon the porridge was bubbling at the top of the pot. But the mother had forgotten the magic words! The porridge kept on rising and began to spill over the rim. "Halt, Little Pot, halt!" the mother said. The porridge only boiled and bubbled over faster. "Enough, Little Pot, enough!" cried the mother, trying to remember the right words.

The porridge flowed down until it covered the floor of the cottage.

The mother struggled to the door and opened it wide to let the porridge flow out of the house. "No more, Little Pot, no more," she shouted. The stream of delicious porridge flowed through the cottage door and onto the street. Down the street ran the mother screaming, "Cease, Little Pot, cease!" But the porridge flowed on and on, toward the very last house in the village where the little girl was visiting.

When the mother reached the house she called, "Help, help! The magic pot keeps boiling, boiling, boiling!" At once the little girl guessed what was wrong. So she waded into the thick, heavy porridge and ran home as fast as she could, with her mother behind her.

When the little girl reached the cottage she cried, "Stop, Little Pot, stop! Stop, Little Pot, stop! Stop, Little Pot, stop! Stop, Little Pot, stop!" And the magic pot stopped boiling.

Then everyone in the village came out into the street carrying dippers, spoons, cups, bowls, buckets, platters, pans, plates, and pitchers. They dipped up the porridge and they scooped up the porridge, and they spooned up the porridge. There was enough porridge for everyone to feast on for days and days.

After that, the little girl and her mother and the people of the village never went hungry. But they never forgot the words to stop the magic pot from boiling. "Stop, Little Pot, stop!"

DATABANK · STORY

Martin Luther King

Got me a special place
For Martin Luther King.
His picture on the wall
Makes me sing.

I look at it for a long time
And think of some
Real good ways
We will overcome.

MYRA COHN LIVINGSTON

Valentine Feelings

I feel flippy,
I feel fizzy,
I feel whoopy,
I feel whizzy.

I'm feeling wonderful.
I'm feeling just fine.
Because you just gave me
A valentine.

LEE BENNETT HOPKINS

284

Labor Day

Packing
up her picnic,
pouring cold lemonade
in the park grass, Summer says
good-bye!

MYRA COHN LIVINGSTON

October

In October
I'll be host
to witches, goblins
and a ghost.
I'll serve them
chicken soup
on toast.
Whoopy once
whoopy twice
whoopy chicken soup
with rice.

MAURICE SENDAK

Rhyme

I like to see a thunder storm,
    A dunder storm,
      A blunder storm,
I like to see it, black and slow,
Come stumbling down the hills.

I like to hear a thunder storm,
    A plunder storm,
      A wonder storm,
Roar loudly at our little house
And shake the window sills!

ELIZABETH COATSWORTH

Cynthia in the Snow

It SUSHES.
It hushes
The loudness in the road.
It flitter-twitters,
And laughs away from me.
It laughs a lovely whiteness,
And whitely whirs away,
To be
Some otherwhere,
Still white as milk or shirts.
So beautiful it hurts.

GWENDOLYN BROOKS

286

Who Has Seen the Wind?

Who has seen the wind?
    Neither I nor you:
But when the leaves hang trembling,
    The wind is passing through.
Who has seen the wind?
    Neither you nor I:
But when the leaves bow down their heads,
The wind is passing by.

CHRISTINA ROSSETTI

Necks

The swan has a neck that is curly and long.
The camel has one that is shaggy and strong.
But the spotted giraffe
Has a neck and a half.

ROWENA BENNETT

A Monkey

He likes to sit
With head in hand
   Upon his little shelf,
A feeling I
Can understand.
   I think a lot myself.

MARCHETTE CHUTE

Here She Is

Jungle necklaces are hung
Around her tiger throat
And on her tiger arms are slung
Bracelets black and brown;
She shows off when she lies down
All her tiger strength and grace,
You can see the tiger blaze
In her tiger eyes, her tiger face.

MARY BRITTON MILLER

Mathematics on the Job

You need good math skills for many different jobs.

A bank teller uses math. A teller must add, subtract, multiply, and divide. A teller must be able to count money. A teller uses math skills all day long.

An architect plans new buildings. Architects help to build homes, stores, and skyscrapers. Architects use math skills to help them measure. They also use math to figure out how strong building materials must be.

A computer programmer uses math skills every day. To make a computer work, a programmer must tell it what to do. Computer programmers often use math in the programs they write.

Insurance agents use math on the job. They sell many different kinds of insurance. They must figure out what kind of insurance a person needs. Then they must find out how much the insurance will cost.

Picture Halves

You know that two halves make one whole. Did you know that two halves can make one picture?

Put some drops of paint on the fold of a piece of paper. Close the paper and press along the fold. When you open the paper, you will see a lovely design. The fold of the paper divides the design into *two halves*.

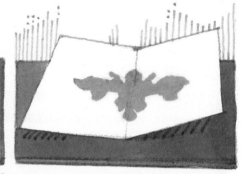

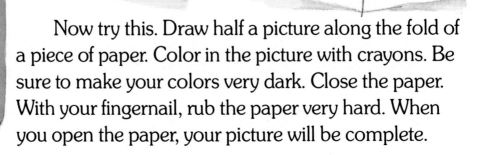

Now try this. Draw half a picture along the fold of a piece of paper. Color in the picture with crayons. Be sure to make your colors very dark. Close the paper. With your fingernail, rub the paper very hard. When you open the paper, your picture will be complete.

292

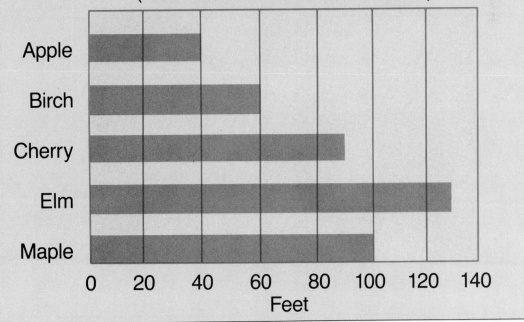

Tree Champions

Every year, the American Forestry Association makes a list of the largest trees in the United States. They have been doing this for almost 50 years. It helps people to learn more about trees of all sizes. Many people have become interested in hunting for very tall trees. They look for large trees and report them to the Forestry Association. Michigan has 75 national champion trees. Florida has 99. California has 68.

The tallest tree in the country is a California redwood. It is 362 feet tall. This tree is 57 feet taller than the Statue of Liberty! Tree-hunters continue to search for new champions.

Some of the Biggest Trees in America
(Rounded to the Nearest Ten Feet)

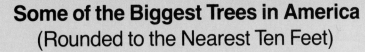

Apple

Birch

Cherry

Elm

Maple

0   20   40   60   80   100   120   140
Feet

Making a Musical Shaker

Musical Instruments

Bass
- String instrument
- Can be played with bow or plucked with fingers
- Deep sound

Clarinet
- Wind instrument
- Both hands move keys to change sounds
- Makes high, sharp sounds and lower, softer sounds

French Horn
- Brass instrument
- One hand moves keys to change sounds
- Makes clear, strong sounds; can make soft sounds

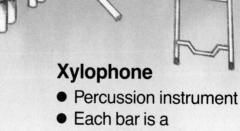

Xylophone
- Percussion instrument
- Each bar is a different sound
- Hit with mallets
- Clear sound

Fish Magic by Paul Klee

Detail Paul Klee, "Fish Magic"
Courtesy of the
Philadelphia Museum of Art:
The Louise and Walter Arensberg
Collection

The Mountains

mountain peak

mountain lion

bear

mountain laurel

mountain goat

snow

snowshoe rabbit

mountain beaver

The Beach

cove

lobster

seaweed

seashore

jellyfish

wave

beach grass

mussels

sand dollar

DATABANK: Science **299**

Unusual Pets

People all over the world keep animals as pets. The most popular pets are dogs, cats, parakeets, canaries, and fish.

Some people keep unusual pets. The pictures on these pages show some of them. Unusual pets have special needs. They may eat special kinds of food. They may be awake at times when most people are asleep.

People must think carefully when they decide what kind of pet to keep. How much space the animal will have in a home is one thing to think about. How much care a person can give a pet is another. What kind of unusual pet would you choose?

Macaws are colorful parrots. They eat nuts, seeds, and fruit. They are beautiful to look at. However, they have very sharp beaks. You must be careful not to get bitten.

Wild skunks are known for the bad-smelling liquid they spray when they are scared. Pet skunks usually cannot spray. Their black and white coats are shiny and beautiful. Skunks eat mostly insects and some fruits and grain.

Pigs are often considered dirty animals. In fact, as pets, they are very clean. Pigs are smart, gentle and friendly animals. One pet pig even saved a boy from drowning!

Pigs will eat most foods. They especially like grains, vegetables, and milk. Pigs grow to be very big and usually must be kept outside.

At the Airport

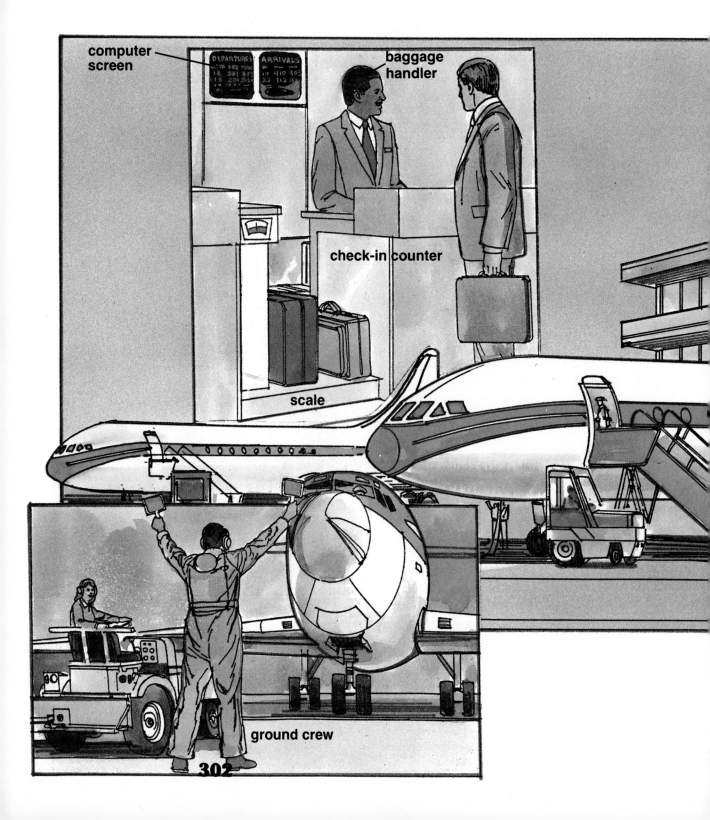

computer
screen

baggage
handler

check-in counter

scale

ground crew

302

control tower

radar screen

traffic controller

headphones

terminal

porter

luggage cart

walkie-talkie

guard

DATABANK · PICTURE ESSAY

Harvest Festivals

Many cities and towns in our country have harvest festivals. A harvest festival is a celebration that is held after a crop has been gathered. Everyone is glad that the hard work of picking the crop and taking it to market is over. The photographs on these pages show some of the harvest festivals that are held in different parts of the country.

A festival called Husker Harvest Days is held in Grand Island, Nebraska, each September.

The Cordele Watermelon Festival takes place every July in Cordele, Georgia.

In Pella, Iowa, a festival called Tulip Time is held every year in May.

The Grape Jamboree is a festival held in Geneva, Ohio, each September.

John Muir

Muir Woods is a large area of tall redwood trees. It is located near San Francisco, California. Muir Woods is named after John Muir.

John Muir spent his life studying nature. He traveled all over the United States and to many other parts of the world. It was Muir's dream to explore places that people had never seen before. He explored areas in the Arctic. He traveled to the western frontier on foot. There he lived alone in the Yosemite Valley in the Sierra Nevada mountains.

He decided to make the Yosemite Valley his home. He studied the beautiful valley. He was the first person to discover how the valley was created. It had been formed by large masses of ice called **glaciers.**

John Muir is best known for his fight to preserve America's wilderness areas. He asked President Theodore Roosevelt to set aside land for two large national parks.

Because of John Muir, Yosemite and Sequoia National Parks were created. Because of his work, John Muir is known as the "father of our national parks."

INDEX